New Hampshire's Most Scenic Roads

NEW HAMPSHIRE'S MOST *scenic* ROADS

22 Routes Off the Beaten Path

John Gibson

Photographs by the author
Maps by Ruth Ann Hill

DOWN EAST BOOKS

ISBN 0-89272-513-3
LCCN: 2001087618

Designed by Phil Schirmer
Printed and bound at Versa Press, Inc.

2 4 6 8 9 7 5 3 1

DOWN EAST BOOKS
P.O. Box 679
Camden, Maine 04843
book orders: 1-800-766-1670

Remembering

Bessie Gibson

1901-2001

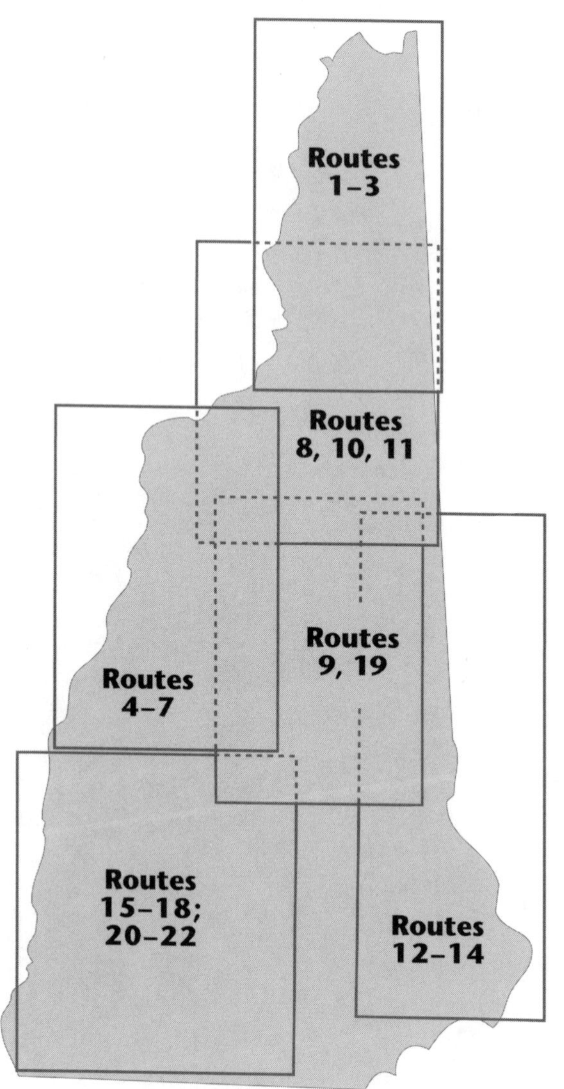
Routes
1–3
Routes
8, 10, 11
Routes
4–7
Routes
9, 19
Routes
15–18;
20–22
Routes
12–14

contents

Southeast and Seacoast

Southwestern–Monadnock Region

West-Central Region

Acknowledgments

Appendixes

An Introduction

When Thornton Wilder conjured up Grovers Corners, he was thinking about New Hampshire, and a good thing, too. New Hampshire, the rock-ribbed Granite State, serves up inviting rural countryside that beckons the turnpike-weary traveler in a way that few states do. It's a state of good people and charming small towns—much like Wilder imagined, only better.

From its beginnings in the southeast—in coastal Portsmouth, Rye, Hampton, and Exeter—to the lofty peaks of New Hampshire's White Mountains along the spine of the great Appalachian chain, then westward to the captivating hill country of Hillsborough, Sullivan, and Cheshire Counties, New Hampshire offers back-roads explorers a collection of colorful byways that remain a pleasure to drive and a treat for the eye, as well as comfortable places to stop and rest awhile. Whether or not you'll discover characters such as those whom Wilder fathomed in *Our Town* is left for each traveler to speculate. But, certainly, the open road is yours.

Motorists will find New Hampshire an appealing destination throughout the four seasons. The state is a summer playground of beautiful lakes and country fairs, a winter center of alpine and cross-country skiing, a place of open harbors and green college lawns come spring, and of highways bordered by spectacular autumn color. This state *enjoys* playing host, too, and a variety of centers provide welcoming accommodations, a choice of restaurants, and other diversions, all against a backdrop of unforgettable landscapes.

Until recently, New Hampshire remained a rocky-pastured, rural state untouched by the trends of modern living and visible to many in America only every four years, when it hosts its first-in-the-nation presidential primary. Peopled by those whom Cornelius Weygandt called "the merriest of Puritans," it was, and in many ways still is, a state that finds its best descriptors in tales of wild men such as Jigger Johnson, who worked its northern forests and lived rough; in the pages of Robert Frost's poetry; in the exploits of men such as Darby Field, who first climbed Mount Washington in 1642; and in the remarkable legends of its small hill towns, villages, and impressive mountains.

Despite yielding its southernmost turf to the kind of modern development seen nearly everywhere in America, with high-density housing and electronics-age industry spilling over the border from Massachusetts, New Hampshire is still blessed with some of the most appealing natural countryside in America. This book concentrates on the scenic roads in the less-developed areas, where the flavor of a state rich in beautiful countryside still firmly maintains.

New Hampshire abounds in lakes, streams, and mountains. Travelers will find much to do outdoors, and driving the scenic roads described in this guide will transport you to dozens of the state's most appealing natural places. Some of the routes included here traverse impressive mountain valleys locked between the Northeast's highest mountain ranges. Other drives skirt those ranges, to follow circular routes around dozens of peaks in the state's northern precincts. Some chase the seacoast and its history. Several routes wander the rolling farm country and timberland that occupy the west and southwest of the state, and still other pages of this book send you alongside such great New Hampshire rivers as the Connecticut, the Ammonoosuc, and the Androscoggin. All of the routes contained in this book are designed to meander, not to get you somewhere in a hurry. A leisurely pace, allowing time to stop and visit many points of interest, is encouraged. The appealing beauty of the New Hampshire countryside deserves your full attention. Absolutely.

New Hampshire's Most Scenic Roads provides exact directions to the most attractive rural highways and back roads. Each route is described in detail, with notes on natural and man-made attractions. Photographs give you an idea of what you'll see. All journeys described in this volume include an easy-to-read map. You may also wish to carry larger maps as you travel. The *New Hampshire Atlas and Gazetteer* makes a good companion, as does the *Rand McNally Road Atlas*.

In *New Hampshire's Most Scenic Roads*, history buffs will find sites to visit such as the Daniel Webster birthplace, the Franklin Pierce Homestead, and the Willey House Slide. Fanciers of things antique or of fine colonial, Federal, and Greek Revival architecture will discover much to please: the Civil War waterfront warehouses of Portsmouth, the period architecture of well-preserved shire towns such as Claremont, the lovely campus buildings of Dartmouth College, and the picturesque old capes and saltboxes of Center

Sandwich. Culture mavens will be reminded to visit such outstanding points as Dartmouth's Hopkins Center, Manchester's Currier Gallery of Art (which boasts the only Frank Lloyd Wright–designed home open to the public in New England), and the University of New Hampshire's Paul Arts Center.

If activity and fresh air are your preference, you'll find that New Hampshire offers nearly unlimited resources in every region of the state. If you like hiking, cycling, or fishing, you'll find numerous indicators in this book on where you might stretch your legs or limber up your rod and reel. Hiking-trail networks and camping areas are also referenced, and numerous opportunities for boating are noted.

Early Beginnings

New Hampshire saw English exploration as early as 1603 with the wanderings of Captain Martin Pring at the mouth of the Piscataqua River. Samuel de Champlain apparently sailed along the New Hampshire coast two years later, followed by Captain John Smith in 1614. In 1620, King James I officially established the Plymouth Colony, a vast land grant that included the region now known as New Hampshire. A Captain Mason became the grantee of the territory in 1622. Settlement first occurred at Odiorne Point, in what is now Rye, in 1623, and Dover became the seat of the first formally established local government in 1633. Coastal settlements grew as Exeter and Hampton were established in 1638 and 1639, respectively. Needing administrative structure, New Hampshire became a district of Massachusetts in 1641.

Ignorance and foresight coexisted. Quakers were whipped or hanged in the territory in the mid-1600s for their religious beliefs while more visionary, tolerant men voted to help fund Harvard College, whence came many of New England's early clergy. In 1685, New Hampshire became part of the Province of New England, then achieved separate provincial status again in 1691. Conflicts with Native Americans arose and came to a head in King Philip's War, between 1689 and 1697. Scottish-Irish immigrants began settling inland New Hampshire in places such as Londonderry in 1719. Renewed hostilities with Indians culminated in Lovewell's War and the Battle of Lovewell's Pond in 1725. Thirty-eight towns had been chartered in the province by 1732, but the population remained small. Governor Benning Wentworth became royal governor in 1741 and began an energetic development of the province, granting seventy-five township charters during his administration.

By 1761, stagecoach service linked Boston and Portsmouth, though waterborne coastal passage remained preferable. In 1764, New Hampshire's western boundary was fixed, and the last royal governor to oversee these lands, John Wentworth, gained appointment in 1767. By 1770, New Hampshire was divided into five counties. In 1774, Fort William and Mary in New Castle was seized and occupied by revolutionary patriots, who renamed it Fort Constitution. Portsmouth supplied ships to the struggle, and New Hampshire privateers harassed British shipping effectively. The province declared itself independent of Britain in January 1776, though its western communities did not subscribe to the new state constitution until 1782.

Getting Ready to Travel

New Hampshire yields to investigation via two major north-south routes: Interstate 93 (I-93) and NH 16 (sometimes known as the Spaulding Turnpike in its southern section). The interstate, more pleasant than most superhighways, winds up the center, then west center of the state, into the Franconia Range country. Traveling through the heart of New Hampshire's western mountains, it then curves farther westward toward the state line and Vermont's Northeast Kingdom.

NH 16 travels from coastal Portsmouth to a point more than 150 miles to the north in the Magalloway watershed, above Umbagog Lake, where it crosses into Maine. Although NH 16 has been overtaken by development in many spots, in other places it is a lovely road. Once a rural highway of surpassing beauty, especially as it approaches the mountains, NH 16 is now an often crowded road, sometimes lined with billboards and hideous commercial outlets of every stripe. This road debouches into a once-serene intervale in the heart of "Mount Washington Valley," lately the scene of malls, bargain outlets, motels, and fast-food joints. Ironically, this spoiled valley floor, bordered by the majestically fine Moat Range to the west, was once revered for its unique beauty and became a favorite motif of prominent painters of the White Mountain School such as Albert Bierstadt. No more.

I recommend using either of these roads only as a means of getting to some of the quieter and more attractive routes listed in these pages. Drivers should be aware that in high summer, in ski season, and again during the autumn foliage season, both roads, especially NH 16, may see heavy traffic. Use I-93 and NH 16 merely as ladders for a quick climb upstate, then jump off onto the lovely rural roads mentioned here; they are the most scenic in New Hampshire.

Travelers seeking to cross the state will find that the major east-west connector in the south is NH 101, which efficiently links the seacoast region to midstate Manchester and I-93. In northern New

Hampshire, US 2 traverses the state in mountain country from picturesque Shelburne to Littleton. From midstate Concord, the state capital, I-89 runs northwestward through attractive countryside to Lebanon-Hanover and thence to Vermont. I-89 moves through entirely rural countryside, going around many attractive little villages worth a stop; except for the section immediately west of Bow, the highway is rarely crowded. Even NH 16, once north of Berlin, becomes again a scenic, pleasant road on which to drive to the state's northern limits.

Using This Guide

For descriptive purposes, this book divides the state into six regions. The first region—**North Country**—covers mountainous northern New Hampshire, or Coos County. **Western New Hampshire** encompasses the western mountains and upper Connecticut River zone in Grafton County. The **White Mountains** drives emphasize the spectacular Eastern Slopes area. The fourth region, **Southeast and Seacoast New Hampshire**, provides routes in Rockingham, Strafford, and Carroll Counties, to the southeast, in or near coastal New Hampshire. The **Southwestern and Monadnock** routes lie in Sullivan, Cheshire, Merrimack, and Hillsborough Counties, to the southwest. The **West Central New Hampshire** drives explore the pretty west-central hill country. This volume describes the point-to-point routes or circuits that provide the most scenic, interesting driving in each region.

Amenities

In New Hampshire, the availability of motorist services varies with the region. In the north country, North Woodstock, North

Conway, Littleton, Berlin, and Colebrook are the most populous centers and can be expected to offer motorist services from morning until midevening. In southern and central New Hampshire—Portsmouth, Rochester, Manchester, Concord, Keene, and Lebanon-Hanover—services are reliably available throughout the day and evening, and sometimes overnight. Small towns in the backcountry are less likely to have fuel or food service in the evenings or overnight. Many New Hampshire businesses are strongly influenced by seasonal tourism, and roadside services may be less available in the off seasons. Because this book actively invites you to get away from major arteries and into the backcountry, you should expect to see fewer services on these attractive rural roads and plan for fuel, maintenance, accommodations, and dining accordingly. If you are vacationing from out of state, you may find it comfortable to establish a base in a region, drive the routes described here without hurrying, and return to your central base each evening.

Advance planning is highly desirable to ensure your comfort while traveling, especially on holiday weekends, in foliage season, and during the ski months. Small inns and campgrounds, for example, tend to fill up early. Travelers will find that some communities support their own local tourist information center, useful for last-minute arrangements and local directions.

All Outdoors

Opportunities for hiking, cycling, camping, fishing, hunting,skiing, and boating are numerous in New Hampshire. Regional tourist centers and state agencies can provide information. There are sixty-nine state parks and state forests in New Hampshire, many offering camping facilities or other recreational opportunities. Travelers also may wish to contact the New Hampshire Division of Travel and Tourism and the New Hampshire Department of Fish and Game for information on accommodations, fishing and hunting, and specialized sports such as skiing and cycling. Both agencies are located in Concord, New Hampshire. The Appalachian Mountain Club (AMC), formed in 1876, is an excellent information resource for hiking, particularly in New Hampshire's magnificent White Mountains. The AMC operates a high hut system in the northern mountains and other hiking-related facilities open to the public in different parts of the state. The AMC's operational center and hiker accommodations are located on NH 16 in Pinkham Notch, at the eastern trailhead to Mount Washington. District rangers for the extensive White Mountain National Forest are also located on this road, farther north in Gorham. Outfitters for hiking and backpacking can be found in North Conway, Intervale, and North Woodstock.

Art and Antiques

Those with a cultural bent may wish to combine scenic drives with visits to New Hampshire's active cultural centers. Keene, Portsmouth-Exeter, Hanover-Lebanon, Concord, and Manchester often play host to major cultural events and are home to theaters, galleries, and exhibits. Granite State educational centers, such as the University of New Hampshire in Durham (with system campuses in Keene, Plymouth, and Manchester), often host significant cultural and artistic programs. Dartmouth College's Hopkins Center and Hood Museum of Art, in Hanover, and several private schools, such as Phillips Exeter Academy, also present various cultural programs, recitals, and exhibits. Manchester's excellent Currier Gallery of Art regularly mounts shows of high artistic merit and cultural relevance and holds originals by Copley, Monet, Constable, Picasso, Bierstadt, Hassam, and Hopper, among others, in its collections.

The League of New Hampshire Craftsmen, with regional exhibits and retail centers, presents the work of highly talented contemporary craftspeople and artists. Numerous small, local galleries and private foundations and institutions host a variety of seasonal exhibits; travelers should check local schedules for these often interesting events. Leading educational institutions provide seasonal programs in drama and film, and there are a number of regional summer theater productions and music series. Local guides and newspapers publish information and schedules for these offerings.

New Hampshire is a kind of mecca for people who enjoy antiques. The state has more than its share of dealers scattered along country roads and in collectives, where many dealers cooperate. Travelers should keep their eye on Manchester, where for nearly forty-five years large numbers of antique merchants and collectors have come together every August for sales and other events. Check local announcements for this antiques fanciers' celebration.

The "Off" Season

To many, New Hampshire's scenic roads seem just as attractive in the winter months. An engaging Currier and Ives landscape unfolds in winter, when the northern mountains become more than spectacular, clothed in snow and brilliant light. The rolling hills and hill farms of western New Hampshire in winter, wrapped in a perfect white coverlet, make for rewarding off-season drives. Nordic ski enthusiasts will find several extensive trail networks to visit, and downhill skiers will discover plenty to challenge them at New

Hampshire's major downhill centers. Back roads are usually well plowed, and fireside accommodations are welcoming at the end of the day in the winter season, when competition for accommodations is less than in high summer.

New Hampshire Terrain

Anyone driving New Hampshire's rural routes will have reason to remark on the exceptional geology of this region. New Hampshire rests on old plutonic and sedimentary rock, particularly the former, which has been upthrust, then weathered profoundly over millennia. The state is traversed by a great spine of raised rock from south-west to northeast, one of the most striking sections of the entire Appalachian cordillera. Granodiorites, particularly in the Littleton and Conway formations, dominate the great White Mountain highlands. The Presidential Range itself rises on the backs of great deposits of schists and gneiss. Bands of slates and quartzites underlay the coastal zone. Conglomerate schists, slates, other sedimentary rocks, and pegmatitic deposits shape the valleys of the Connecticut River region. And everywhere, there are the hills.

New Hampshire's mountains are very old, their rounded, bold shapes the result of weathering of ancient plains into peaks and valleys. These same mountains also show the effects of massive glaciation during the last ice age, when the state was covered by a mile-thick ice sheet. Glacial ice dominated New Hampshire beginning about twenty-one thousand years ago, then slowly retreated and has been absent now for roughly eleven thousand years. New Hampshire's mountains were liberally scraped by the moving glacial ice, and there are many examples of typical glacial effects along the ridgelines of the state's most impressive mountains. The Great Gulf, for example, located on the east side of the northern Presidential Range, between Mount Washington and Mounts Clay, Jefferson, and Adams, is a perfect example of a raised glacial cirque. A walk beneath the north side of Mount Washington's summit reveals examples of the glacial feature known as polygon bodens. Glacial tarns and bogs, and hillsides showing glacial plucking, are common features of New Hampshire geology, too. Such terrain is ever compelling to the eye.

The highest ridges of these same glaciated mountains are also host to species of vegetation native to more northerly climates. On the cold summit highlands in the Presidentials around Mount Washington, for example, the hiker will come across plants that are more commonly found in northern Labrador, as well as subarctic insect species whose entire adult life span is a matter of only a few hours.

Many features of the glaciated countryside are visible as one drives the back roads. Other features can be glimpsed best by pulling off the road and hiking to them. Several drives described in this volume take the traveler directly through mountain country, and networks of hiking trails transport those who enjoy outdoor walks into the heart of this unusual geology and plant life. Walkers can connect whole regions of alpine geology, flora, and fauna. Some trails are arduous; others are appropriate for even the inexperienced. *Always get information locally before you hike.*

Getting Ready

Travelers who plan to navigate New Hampshire's back roads in search of both scenery and history may want first to head to the library or old-books store to get a sense of the territory. Mountain hikers will enjoy perusing Daniel Ford's engaging *The Country Northward*, a fine chronicle of a walking journey in the White Mountains, or Robert Pike's *Spiked Boots*, a compelling reminiscence of life in the state's northern logging camps. Charles E. Clark's *The Eastern Frontier: The Settlement of Northern New England, 1610–1763*, is a first-class history of America's *other* frontier in colonial days. Consult a library for the most detailed classic compendium of the state in five volumes, Hobart Pillisbury's 1927-issue *New Hampshire Resources, Attractions, and Its People*. Francis Belcher's *Logging Railroads of the White Mountains* (1980) is an interesting history of the little railroads that crisscrossed New Hampshire's Pemigewasset Wilderness in the days when men were misguidedly intent on cutting it all down. One gets a penetrating sense of rural New Hampshire in the poems of Donald Hall and his captivating essay collections *Here at Eagle Pond* and *Seasons at Eagle Pond*.

Two classic histories of the White Mountains are Thomas Starr King's *The White Hills* (1860) and Cornelius Weygandt's *White Hills: Mountain New Hampshire* (1934). Both may be found at used-book dealers and in libraries. Donald D. Keyes's *The White Mountains: Place and Perceptions* (1980) is an indispensable introduction to artists who have taken New Hampshire as their subject matter. Harry Scheiber's *Abbot-Downing and the Concord Coach* (1989) tells of New Hampshire's primary connection to elsewhere in the days before railroads. For an exhaustive and delightful account of the Northeast's highest mountain, read F. Alan Burt's *Mount Washington* (1960). A colorful rendition of early travels and tourism in New Hampshire is Charles Stuart Lane's *First Tourists*, available at the Old Print Barn in Meredith and in bookstores. For a visual reconnoiter of

New Hampshire before you arrive, see Peter Randall's *New Hampshire: Photographs* (1979).

For hikers, Daniel Doan's *50 Hikes in the White Mountains* and *Fifty More Hikes in New Hampshire* are essential. Also highly useful is the Appalachian Mountain Club (AMC) *White Mountain Guide*; AMC hiking maps are available in many stores throughout the state, particularly in the mountain regions.

Travelers will find *The Official New Hampshire Hospitality Guide*, *The Official New Hampshire Guidebook*, and *The Official New Hampshire Lodging and Restaurant Guide* useful. They're available from the New Hampshire Division of Travel and Tourism, P.O. Box 1856, Concord, New Hampshire 03302-1856, or you can check on-line at www.visitnh.gov.

A Modest Proposal

In an age of scarce fuel, high gasoline prices, and long-overdue sensitivity to air quality, it makes sense to take a few steps to make motoring more fuel efficient and nonpolluting. Get your car tuned up. Make sure your tires are correctly inflated, for safety and comfort and to reduce rolling resistance and boost fuel economy. Do your touring in a vehicle smaller and more fuel efficient than a river barge. Drive at a sensible, unhurried pace. New Hampshire awards no prizes for drivers who exceed the speed limit, and a friendly state trooper may seek a conversation with you if you do. And remember, rural roads are not superhighways; you may encounter the unexpected (and immovable) just around the next bend.

As I noted in the companion guide to this volume, *Maine's Most Scenic Roads*, true enjoyment of rural roads comes about only if you slow down, relax, take time to stop at interesting places, get off the highway to enjoy natural and cultural sites, and otherwise combat the silly American impulse to rush everywhere. Plan your trip, set aside enough time, and be flexible with your schedule. Visitor or native, you'll find pleasant days and much to enjoy along New Hampshire's scenic rural roads.

Most drives in this book make occasional reference to distance traveled as a means to helping you find your way. Travelers will find it helpful to set their car's odometer to zero at the point where they begin the route described in each section.

1

Route:

North Country Ways: Berlin to Colebrook

Highway:

Routes 110, 110A, 16, 26

Distance:

49.5 miles (one way)

This journey begins in Berlin, a small northern city locked in a circle of mountains above New Hampshire's highest ranges. The state's most populous northern community, Berlin is the stepping-off place for several attractive drives in New Hampshire's sparsely settled, gemlike north country.

First settled in 1821, Berlin grew out of lands in the region once known as Maynesborough, from a colonial grant. Thomas Lary and Thomas Green established a logging camp here in 1825. Logging, pulp processing, and papermaking have made this spot at the head of the notch a center of settlement and commerce for more than a century. The city is surrounded by low mountains (Mount Carberry, Jericho Mountain, Mount Jasper, and Mount Forest); its southerly backdrop is the even higher mountains of the bold Presidential Range.

Berlin straddles the fast-flowing Androscoggin River, source of water and power for the city's great mills and once the major mode for transport of pulp logs to the paper mills. The city is home to a sizable population of Franco-Americans, whose language and culture dominate the community and who have a long-standing connection with lumbering and work in the mills. Though remote, this small, colorful city had its own symphony orchestra as early as 1926, and it has long been the home of the Nansen Ski and Outing Club, famous for its skiing and snowshoeing competitions, born of the traditions of Berlin's small Scandinavian population.

To travel an interesting and scenic arc northwestward to Colebrook, from the intersection of Green and Pleasant Streets in downtown Berlin, *join NH 110* as it runs west alongside the St. Lawrence and Atlantic Railroad tracks. With ledgy Mount Forest to the left and Mount Jasper to the right, the road runs first through a built-up business area, then, after two miles, follows the valley of Jericho Brook and the Dead River in varied rural countryside, a sharp contrast to the busy city just left behind. Continuing northwest, the route passes between Jericho Lake and Head Pond, four miles from Berlin. To the west and northwest are the many imposing high peaks of the Kilkenny Mountains and the Pilot Range, all part of the northernmost section of the White Mountain National Forest. Views back toward the Presidential Range occur momentarily.

Six miles out, you climb Hodgdon Hill, opposite Square Mountain and Greens Ledge. Two miles farther—past Nay Pond, with its campground and boat launch—you enter the little hamlet of West Milan. If you thought you were in backcountry already, you will enter still more unspoiled rural woodlands now. You are approaching the heart of northern New Hampshire's Coos County timber country and are about to go deeper.

This northernmost New Hampshire county probably derived its

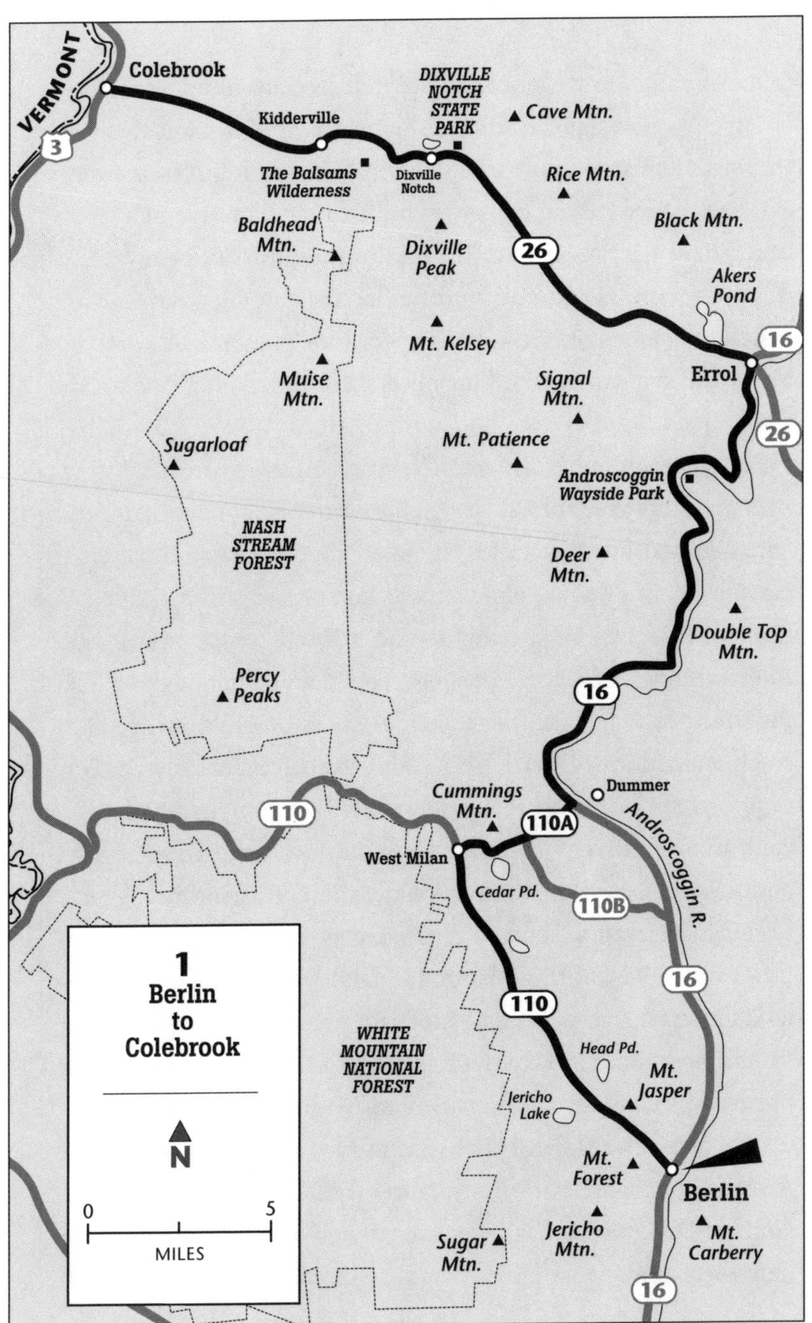

VERMONT
3
Colebrook
Kidderville
DIXVILLE NOTCH STATE PARK
Cave Mtn.
The Balsams Wilderness
Dixville Notch
Rice Mtn.
Black Mtn.
Baldhead Mtn.
Dixville Peak
26
Akers Pond
Mt. Kelsey
16
Errol
Muise Mtn.
Signal Mtn.
26
Sugarloaf
Mt. Patience
Androscoggin Wayside Park
NASH STREAM FOREST
Deer Mtn.
Double Top Mtn.
Percy Peaks
16
Dummer
Cummings Mtn.
110
110A
West Milan
Androscoggin R.
Cedar Pd.
110B
16
1
Berlin
to
Colebrook
110
WHITE MOUNTAIN NATIONAL FOREST
Head Pd.
Mt. Jasper
Jericho Lake
N
Mt. Forest
Berlin
0
5
MILES
Jericho Mtn.
Mt. Carberry
Sugar Mtn.
16

unusual name from one or another interpretation of Indian terms for river or woodland features. The nearby Connecticut River, to the west, contains upper and lower *cohoss*. In local Native American parlance, a *cohoss*, or *coos*, signifies a bend or falls in a riverbed. There are similar river features in the Androscoggin, too, as it flows through this county. Another interpretation is that Coos County is named after the Indian word for pine tree or pinewood; it's a plausible explanation, for pines grow heavily hereabouts and always have.

Beneath Cummings Mountain at West Milan, leave NH 110, *go right and cross* the railroad tracks, *then turn east* on NH 110A toward Dummer and Errol (sign: Milan State Park). You soon drive by appealing Cedar Pond, where you will find camping and boating facilities in otherwise sparsely settled, densely wooded country. After winding in all directions, you pass the junction with NH 110B, pull northeast, and, with Peabody and Closton Hills to the south, reach a junction with NH 16, roughly sixteen miles north of Berlin. Across your dashboard at this junction is the rough-and-tumble Androscoggin River, once the major artery of north-country logging and now an exceptional rapid-water fishery. The Androscoggin begins in the vast watershed of Umbagog Lake, to the north, and flows all the way to the Atlantic in Maine. It is one of New England's greatest rivers, with a history to match.

Turn north on NH 16 (which is pleasantly tranquil up here, well north of its congested section around North Conway) and continue up the map toward Errol. The road curves around a bend in the Androscoggin and works its way eastward in the heavily wooded lands of Dummer, named after an early colonial governor. Along here there is a series of fine river views backed up by mountains in

The upper Androscoggin River

the northern distance. The road is flanked by water through a short section where the river is impounded. You turn north, entering Cambridge twenty miles along, then make your way close to the west side of the Androscoggin, west of Double Top Mountain, Teakettle Ridge, and Jackknife Hill in the Thirteen-Mile Woods. You are likely to see moose, deer, or other wildlife along here, and careful driving is needed. You shortly arrive at Androscoggin Wayside Park. There are many exceptional water views in this lakes region as you drive northward. Keep your eye out for large logging trucks, bound downhill for Berlin.

This is and always has been timber country, where wood is cut both for lumber and to feed the pulp mills in Berlin. The area has played host to a barrel load of characters over the years, including

The Balsams at Abeniki Mountain, Dixville Notch

the notorious Jigger Johnson. He was long thought of as one of the toughest men in the New Hampshire North Woods. He had worked timber since he was a boy and was a river boss by the age of twenty. A feared and respected fighter, he was marked by the blows of at least a hundred fights, most of which he had won.

Johnson worked his men mighty hard, and they sometimes ganged up on him, on one occasion leaving him for dead. His cursing and swearing achieved heights of artistic license that brought far-flung admiration throughout New Hampshire's north country. Jigger Johnson also made his own questionable home brew, which he artfully dubbed "Eagle Sweat." He was reputed to have captured wildcats two at a time and hauled them homeward, one under each arm. The man eventually came to his end by crashing his old Ford into a tree in 1935 while returning drunk one night from Berlin.

The Androscoggin Wayside Picnic Area is twenty-eight miles from your starting point. Errol Hill and Mill Mountain soon become visible to the east, and the road meanders northeast, arriving at the little crossroads of Errol at thirty-four miles. Food and fuel are available here, and it's a good idea to check your fuel gauge; there are few amenities northward between Errol and Colebrook. Restaurants, accommodations, and a sporting goods store are also found at this junction.

At Errol, NH 16 turns farther east for Maine, but you'll *keep left and northwest* on NH 26 toward Dixville Notch and shortly pass by Akers Pond on the right. Through mountainous lands traversed by Corser Brook, Welch Brook, and Clear Stream, the road climbs beneath Signal Mountain and Dixville Peak toward the notch in splendidly wild countryside. The route pulls steadily west as you enter Dixville Notch, below Table Rock, where you'll find another state rest area. NH 26 climbs through the notch amidst interesting bold rock spires that tower jaggedly over the pavement. You then descend to pretty Lake Gloriette. Behind it, on your right, you'll see the striking architecture of The Balsams, one of New Hampshire's premier year-round, full-service resorts, boasting true old-world charm. The starting point of hiking trails to Table Rock and Dixville Peak are on the left side of the road, as is the entrance to The Balsams Wilderness Ski Area.

Crossing the Mohawk River, the road continues westward through the tiny neighborhood of Kidderville. To the south, in Columbia, is Baldhead Mountain; farther are the many small peaks west of Cranberry Notch and Nash Stream Forest. Watch on the right for road access to Coleman State Park, which offers thirty primitive tent sites in the park on the banks of Little Diamond Pond. (There are also RV sites without hookups.) Continuing to follow the Mohawk River, NH 26 rolls westward and, leaving almost unbroken forest, enters the settled part of Colebrook.

Just a stone's throw from the border with Vermont's Essex County, US 3 and NH 26 join in Colebrook, in the shadow of Vermont's big Monadnock Mountain. You'll find restaurants, accommodations, filling stations, and also a small airport here. From Colebrook, adventuresome travelers may wish to continue north to Canada via the beautiful Connecticut Lakes (see next chapter, Route #2), or retrace their travels southeastward along NH 26 and 16, or turn southwest and follow the Vermont border on US 3 toward North Stratford and Lancaster (Route #3, page 39).

2

Route:

The Connecticut Lakes Region: Colebrook to Canada

Highway:

US Route 3, Route 26

Distance:

38.5 miles (one way)

On the map, New Hampshire makes up in height for what it lacks in breadth. At the very top of the Granite State is a wild, mostly unsettled stretch of road that winds through the beautiful Connecticut Lakes to the Canadian border. Travelers on this route are treated to fine, nearly continuous mountain views, abundant rivers, streams, and lakes, and, if desired, entry into the rural countryside of Quebec Province. It is a place of such sublime beauty that other states at times pale by comparison. The region also is completely uncrowded and quiet, there being little to do but enjoy the natural scenery, go birding, fish, hunt, boat, swim, camp, eat well, and relax.

There is but one way open to the Connecticut Lakes, and that is the pleasant drive northward on US 3—a road less traveled, as New Hampshireman Robert Frost put it. The route begins in the interesting, little northern town of Colebrook, the last community of any size from here to Canada. A Colebrook story is told of how a family living near the potato distilleries that long ago were found in this town got in the habit of sending their boy across the road each day for a gallon of "whiskey." Back then, in rural northern New Hampshire, a gallon could be had for a mere twenty-five cents. The proprietor soon grew alarmed at the boy's frequent visits to have his jug refilled, and told the boy so. The lad, admitting no shame at his family's fondness for the brew and determined to carry out his customary errand, remarked, "Hell, what's a gallon of whiskey in a family without a cow?"

From Colebrook center, *take US 3 north* toward West Stewartstown. There are sweeping mountain views as you head out of town; the hills to the west are in Vermont, on the other side of the hidden Connecticut River. Shortly you'll see a state of New Hampshire rest area as the road proceeds through a lovely intervale dotted with farms, some still active. In another three miles, as you pass another farm with dairy herds spread across a hillside and cross the town line of West Stewartstown and, later, Stewartstown, further striking views west to the Vermont hills open up. Seven miles beyond Colebrook you pass through West Stewartstown center and *continue north* on US 3, crossing the forty-fifth parallel and catching an occasional glimpse of the young Connecticut River. The road runs more easterly now in rolling countryside west of Clarksville as the hills close in more tightly.

Thirteen miles above Colebrook, the river appears in an open intervale; three miles farther on, you come to the village of Pittsburg. Watch on the right for a lovely waterfall and the weathered old Pittsburg-Clarksville Bridge over the Connecticut River, opposite the Heath Road marker post. Pass the Pittsburg Historical Society

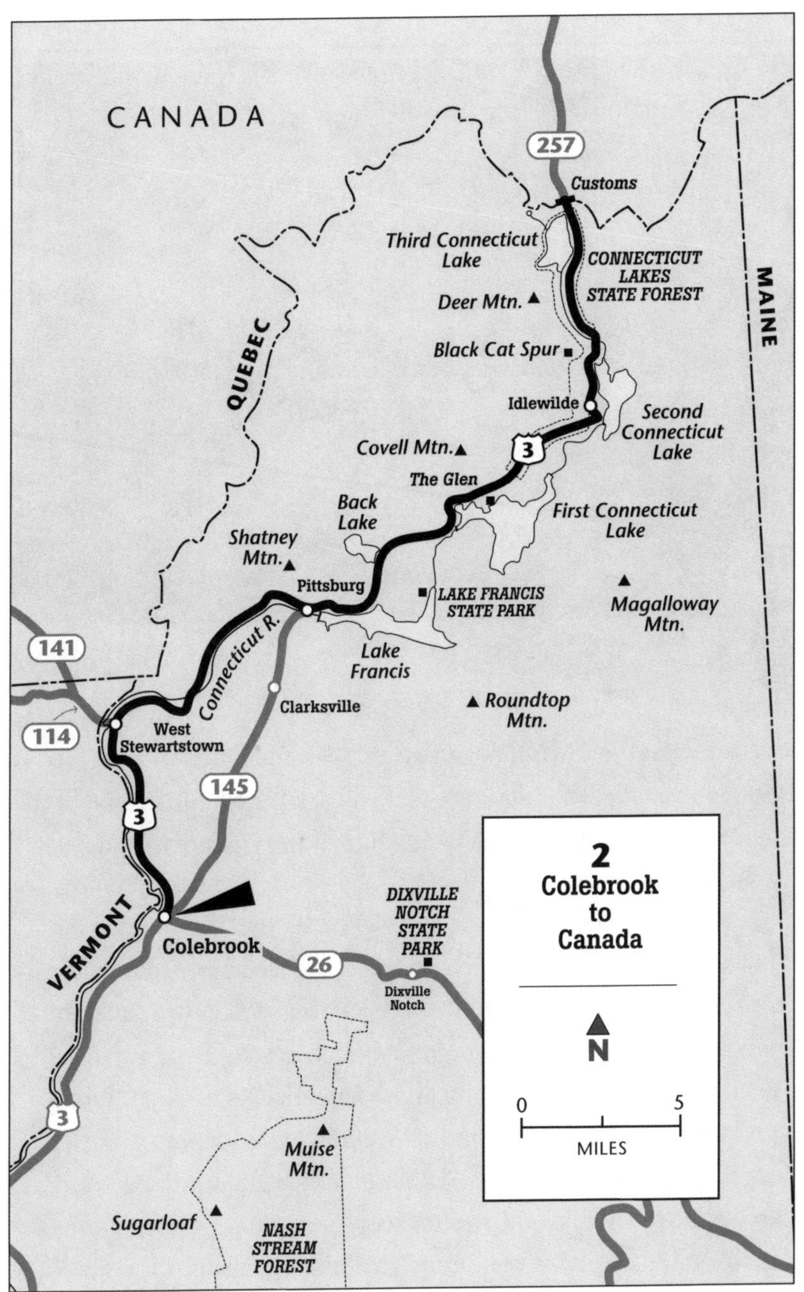
CANADA
257
Customs
Third Connecticut Lake
CONNECTICUT LAKES STATE FOREST
MAINE
QUEBEC
Deer Mtn.
Black Cat Spur
Idlewilde
Second Connecticut Lake
Covell Mtn.
3
The Glen
Back Lake
First Connecticut Lake
Shatney Mtn.
Pittsburg
LAKE FRANCIS STATE PARK
Magalloway Mtn.
141
Connecticut R.
Lake Francis
Clarksville
Roundtop Mtn.
114
West Stewartstown
145
3
VERMONT
Colebrook
26
DIXVILLE NOTCH STATE PARK
Dixville Notch
3
Muise Mtn.
Sugarloaf
NASH STREAM FOREST
2
Colebrook to Canada
N
0
5
MILES

Lake Francis

Museum and the town hall and go through the junction with NH 145. Soon to the right and east you will see Lake Francis, one of the sources of the Connecticut River, which flows hundreds of miles to the sea.

The water views begin now along US 3 by the banks of Lake Francis, and there are public boat launching facilities. Driving northeast, you pass scenic Back Lake off to the left. Watch for River Road on your right; it will take you in to attractive Lake Francis State Park, where there are camping and boating facilities. You'll find a variety of accommodations in this section, including campgrounds, lodges, and sporting camps. Outfitters, tackle shops, and guide services are available. Your route soon comes to the west shore of First Connecticut Lake; the French Wildlife Refuge is on your left, under Covell Mountain. A picnic area overlooks the waters, backed by spectacular mountains across the lake, in Maine.

Twenty-seven miles above Colebrook, you come to Varney Road on the right; it's the entrance to The Glen, one of the oldest and most attractive of the sporting camps along First Connecticut Lake's northwest shore. Beyond Varney Road are superb views eastward over the lake toward Maine, with Magalloway Mountain on the far horizon. Pulling away from the lake, you make a beeline northeastward through the Connecticut Lakes State Forest to Second Connecticut Lake, where you pull northward on US 3 at Idlewilde. There are excellent water views here and opportunities for fishing. Thirty-two miles above Colebrook, you pass the road into Magalloway Mountain Lookout Station. The route climbs, turns, and descends repeatedly along here, with a series of spectacular views, particularly from horizon to horizon to the east.

By Black Cat Spur you descend northward to Deer Mountain Campground, then cross the Connecticut River again while continuing northward within the Connecticut Lakes State Forest. (In the early days, the term *cat* was often applied to small things. People often referred to the small, winding back roads of New Hampshire as "cat roads," and "spurs" were side roads.) You come next to beautiful Third Connecticut Lake, to the west, or left, surrounded by striking, brooding mountains as far as the eye can see. Fishing and boating opportunities are found on these attractive waters.

Just beyond, forty-three miles from Colebrook at the top of a hill, you've run out of United States. Travelers may wish to continue on to the rural Quebec countryside by proceeding through Canadian customs. There are outstanding views northward once you pass through customs, and you may wish to experiment with the "Magnetic Hill," an oddity that will drag your car uphill in seeming defiance of gravity. Or you may head back south, retracing the route to Colebrook and thence southward via Errol to Berlin and the White Mountains. An alternate return southward can be made by following US 3 via West Stewartstown at the Quebec-Vermont border to Groveton, Lancaster, and Littleton for New Hampshire's western mountains and Franconia Range (see next chapter, Route #3).

Note: This region boasts some of the finest fishing in the Northeast. Licenses are available locally, as are tackle and supplies. An Orvis Fly Shop is located in Pittsburg. Most lodges and inns on the water rent canoes, or boats and motors. For those trailering their own boat, a number of lakes have public access points. Inquire locally or at your lodge.

3

Route:

Northern Connecticut River: Colebrook to Lancaster

Highway:

US Route 3

Distance:

37.5 miles (one way)

This route takes you down the Connecticut River and around a series of striking uplands parallel to the Vermont border in northwestern New Hampshire. As you descend the map, you come closer to panoramic views of the highest peaks in the White Mountains. Travel this route as a straightforward scenic river drive, or use it as an alternate return route southward following the first and second journeys described in this book.

From the junction of US 3 and NH 26 in the center of Colebrook, *run southward* on US 3 toward Columbia. The road meanders through a business area, goes by the Notre Dame Sanctuary, then heads into rural country surrounded by low mountains. Monadnock Mountain fades from view on the Vermont side of the river as you pass the Columbia Town Hall. At four miles south of Colebrook, following some railroad tracks in more open country, you'll go by Columbia Bridge Road to Vermont. You may wish to pause and

Covered bridges survive in New Hampshire's remote regions.

view this covered bridge, just a short distance off the main road. Mount Pleasant and Blue, Goback, and Savage Mountains appear ahead on the horizon to the southeast. Inviting views of Vermont hill country open up occasionally to the west.

Stands of thick woodland dominate the landscape, and there is little settlement in this rolling terrain. Occasionally you will glimpse the Connecticut River through the trees below and to the right of the highway.

You cross Lyman Brook and, twelve miles south of Colebrook, pass the junction with VT 105 in North Stratford. There is a beautiful example of New England railroad station architecture here at the bend in the road. US 3, which has been running primarily southwest until now, *turns southeastward* with views into Vermont to Willard, Lake, and Stoneham Mountains as you skirt big Spruce Mountain to the east in New Hampshire. The hills close in here,

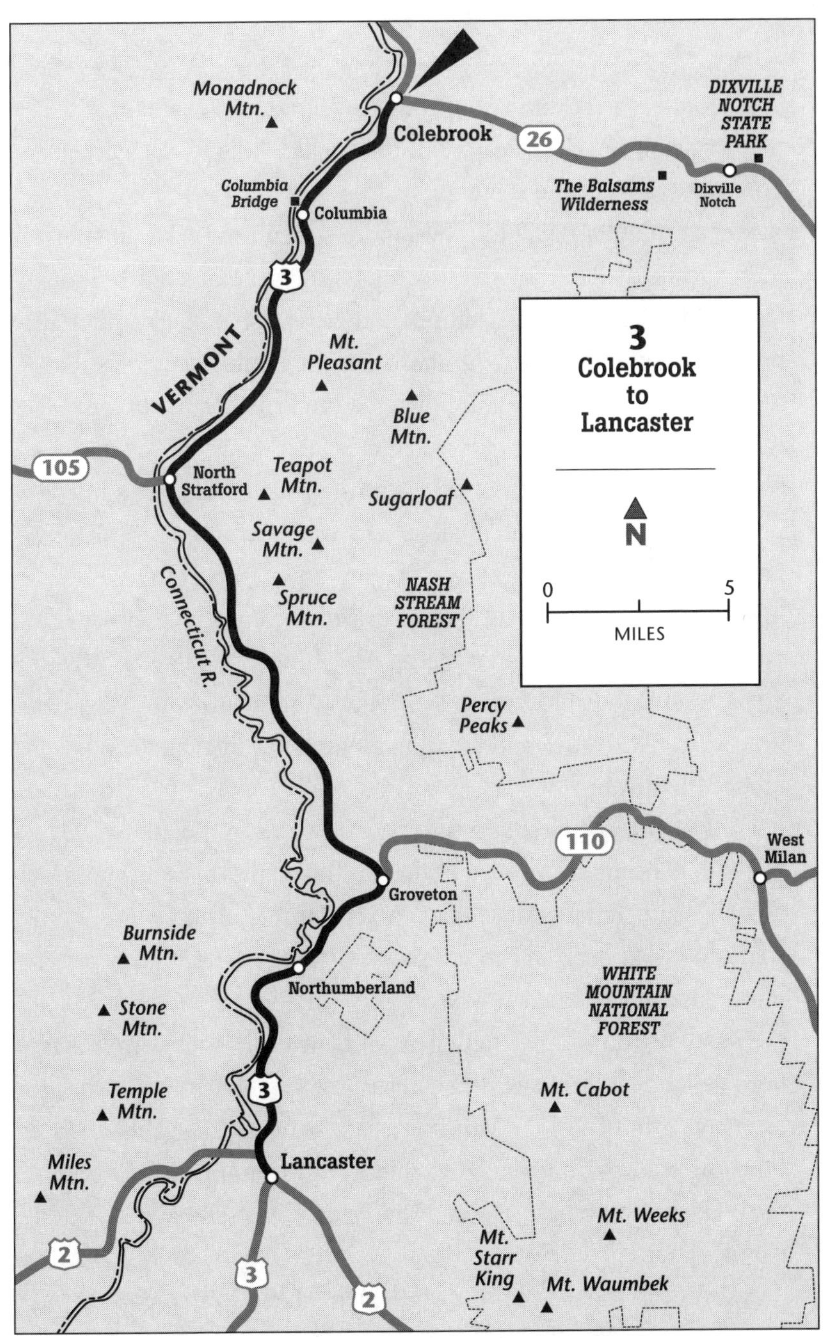
3
Colebrook to Lancaster
N
0
5
MILES
Monadnock Mtn.
Colebrook
26
DIXVILLE NOTCH STATE PARK
The Balsams Wilderness
Dixville Notch
Columbia Bridge
Columbia
3
VERMONT
Mt. Pleasant
Blue Mtn.
105
North Stratford
Teapot Mtn.
Sugarloaf
Savage Mtn.
Spruce Mtn.
NASH STREAM FOREST
Connecticut R.
Percy Peaks
110
West Milan
Groveton
Burnside Mtn.
Northumberland
WHITE MOUNTAIN NATIONAL FOREST
Stone Mtn.
Temple Mtn.
Mt. Cabot
Miles Mtn.
Lancaster
Mt. Weeks
Mt. Starr King
Mt. Waumbek
2
3
2

and soon the great north-south mass of Stratford Mountain and the tangle of the Percy Peaks and the smaller hills of Nash Stream Forest are also seen to the east.

You'll note that the land grows more agricultural now; in summer, cornfields flank the road. You pass the general store at Stratford Hollow, go through a slump, and cross a stream. The intervale broadens out and mountains ahead dot the entire horizon as the road pulls more southeast, following a kind of shelf along the eastern edge of the intervale. You'll cross the Groveton town line twenty-three miles south of your starting point, and crest a hill as US 3 drifts toward town. You'll see the high peaks of the Kilkenny Range ahead. Go through town, staying on US 3 past the Weeks Medical Center, Dartmouth-Hitchcock medical practice, post office, and Groveton United Methodist Church. Follow US 3 (State Street South) toward Lancaster, passing its junction with NH 110 near a covered bridge and crossing a branch of the Upper Ammonoosuc River.

US 3 now bears west and southwest for Northumberland and Guildhall, Vermont. A range of lower hills makes a foreground for Miles and Temple Mountains in Vermont. You turn more southward now, at a bend in the Connecticut River where the land is more built up, yet there are farms and cattle grazing in pastures even as you approach settled areas of Lancaster. Thirty-two miles from Colebrook, you cross the Lancaster town line and pass the extensive grounds of the Lancaster Fair, beneath Page Hill at Coos Junction. Views of a widened Connecticut River appear here and there as you drive past several New Hampshire state agency buildings on your left.

A short distance farther on, you reach a bend in the road by the

Kayakers make their way northward in clear water.

Lancaster Elementary School, where US 3 becomes Main Street. Lancaster is blessed with an attractive main street of shops and other businesses. You'll come soon to the old courthouse on the right, the library, and the post office, where this drive ends. Restaurants, filling stations, and visitor accommodations are located along US 3 and Main Street.

Note: High northwestern New Hampshire and eastern Vermont are in maple-sugar country. Inquire locally in early spring about farms that feature sugaring-off parties. Watching maple syrup being made and tasting fresh syrup are special experiences.

4

Route:

The Upper Valley Region: Hanover to Littleton

Highway:

Route 10

Distance:

61.5 miles (one way)

The Hanover-Lebanon area is a bustling, interesting region on the Connecticut River in western New Hampshire. Hanover is, of course, home to historic Dartmouth College, "the big Green." Nearby Lebanon is a commercial area with an attractive town center wrapped around the imposing commons. Both communities have close links to sister towns across the Connecticut River in Vermont: Hanover to pretty little Norwich, and Lebanon to rapidly growing White River Junction and Hartford.

Hanover sits on raised ground above the Connecticut River, its center intertwined with the Dartmouth College campus. Settled in 1765 by Colonel Edmund Freeman and his family, this town is the site of considerable fine colonial and Georgian architecture, including Dartmouth's marvelous Baker Library. The college green and the Hanover Inn dominate the upper town. Dartmouth itself was founded in 1769 by the Reverend Eleazar Wheelock, who established a college "for the education and instruction of Youth of the Indian Tribes of this land in reading, writing and all parts of learning." The college was named after England's second earl of Dartmouth, a friend of the young institution. As further support, Governor Benning Wentworth presented Dartmouth with large land grants to the northeast in New Hampshire's White Mountains, one of which covered part of lofty Mount Washington.

Attractive country churches line the route north from Hanover.

The University of New Hampshire was first established in Hanover in 1866 as the New Hampshire College of Agriculture and Mechanical Arts; it was later relocated to Durham. Hanover is home to Dartmouth's Hopkins Center, a splendid regional center for the arts with a rotating program of concerts, exhibitions, and studios and very much worth visiting as part of a walking tour of the campus. The Hood Museum of Art boasts some excellent holdings and periodic exhibitions. The nationally respected Dartmouth Medical School is here, too.

Hanover is also home to the Dartmouth Outing Club (DOC), an organization perennially active in river and mountain sports. The famous fifteen-hundred-mile-long Appalachian Scenic Trail, which wends its way from Maine to Georgia, actually passes right through Hanover, and by DOC's back door, as it crosses from

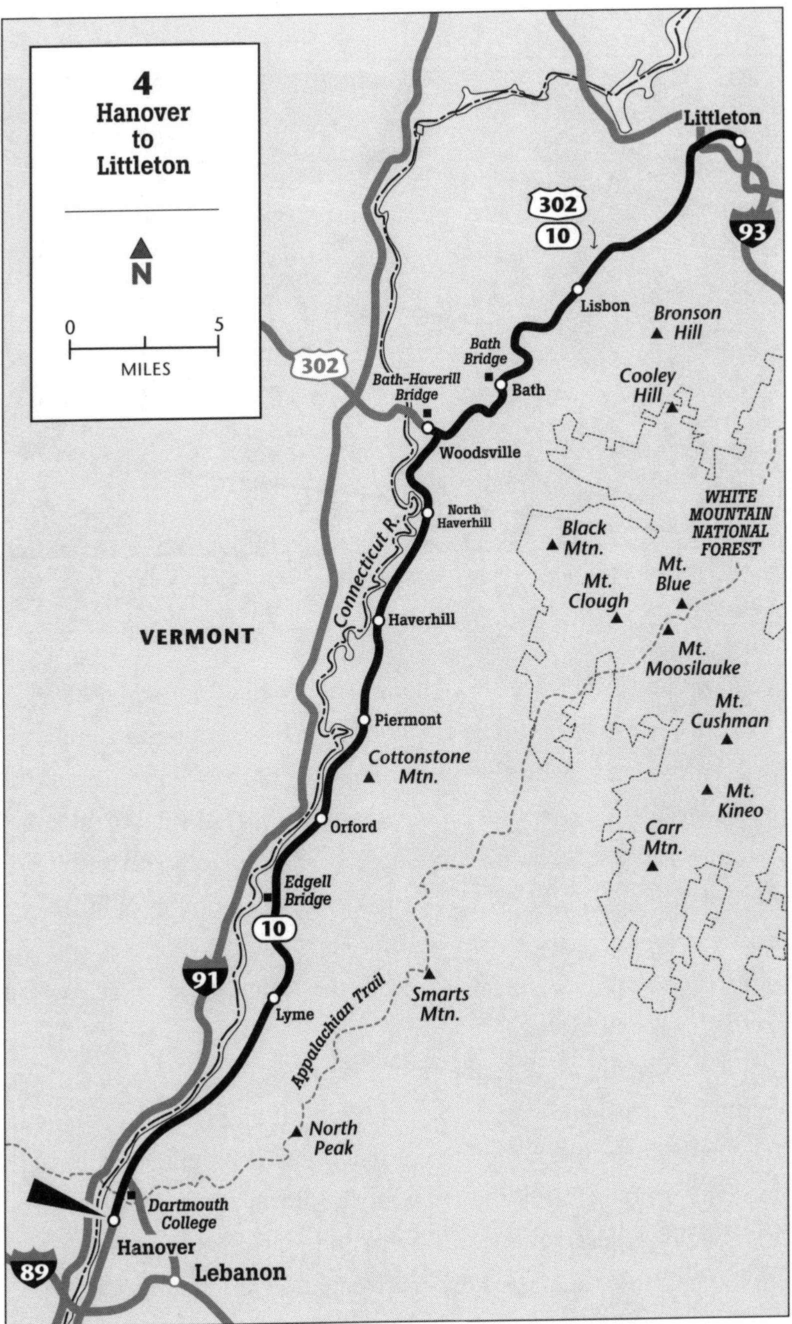

4
Hanover
to
Littleton
N
0
5
MILES
Littleton
302
10
93
Lisbon
Bronson Hill
Bath Bridge
302
Bath-Haverill Bridge
Bath
Cooley Hill
Woodsville
North Haverhill
WHITE MOUNTAIN NATIONAL FOREST
Black Mtn.
Connecticut R.
Mt. Clough
Mt. Blue
Haverhill
VERMONT
Mt. Moosilauke
Piermont
Mt. Cushman
Cottonstone Mtn.
Mt. Kineo
Orford
Carr Mtn.
Edgell Bridge
10
91
Appalachian Trail
Smarts Mtn.
Lyme
North Peak
Dartmouth College
Hanover
89
Lebanon

Handsome architecture fronts the green at Dartmouth College.

Vermont and heads for New Hampshire's White Mountains.

The trip described here is straightforward, beginning in Hanover and making its way northeast up the banks of the Connecticut River into covered-bridge country. From the north side of the Dartmouth campus near the medical school, *take NH 10* (Lyme Road) and head north past Balch and Oak Hills. After passing a number of office centers, the road quickly moves into rural countryside; it goes by Storrs Pond on the right, which feeds the Connecticut River, located to the immediate west.

Pulling slightly more to the northeast, NH 10 runs by lands of the Fullington Trust and passes the point where, on the Vermont side of the Connecticut River, the Ompompanoosuc River enters. Huntington Hill lies immediately to the east. You travel by the Hidden Valley Wildlife Conservation Area soon, and off to the right as you cross Hewes Brook is the Royal C. Nemiah Forest reservation. You head gradually away from the river now, go by Lyme Hill, and cross Grant Brook as you come into the village of Lyme. (A short side trip eastward on Grafton Turnpike brings you to Lyme Center, where there is additional access to the Appalachian Trail.)

Lyme is a handsome village, the first of several encountered on this ride northward. The town has preserved its lovely green, anchored by fine old houses and the lofty Congregational Church, next to a huge carriage shed. This region is still marked with the legacy of old hill farms once common in the area. Here and there, some are still active. In these old farm houses, young couples once conducted furtive courtships under the watchful eyes of family members. As a man sat in the parlor with his chosen young lady, the couple was often separated by jabbering children and others of the household placed there in the name of propriety. So some local young men carried a "courting stick." Actually a long, hollow tube, the stick could be talked into by the young man and listened to, at the other end, by the young lady who had it placed to her ear. Thus, those courting could converse even if they could not sit together. Occasionally, you can find a courting stick in the parlor of an old Lyme home or farmhouse.

From Lyme, continue northward on NH 10, running by Post Pond and Post Pond Preserve, beneath rounded Post Hill. To the west across the Connecticut River are superb views of Vermont countryside. The road now runs parallel to Clay Brook on the left for several miles, after which you will see River Road, also on your left. Pause here briefly, then *head back* along River Road to see the relics of Edgell Bridge, a scenic covered structure above the Clay Brook outflow. Despite various local efforts to preserve such remnants of the past, covered bridges are an endangered species in New

The broad greens of Haverhill invite the traveler.

England because they are prohibitively expensive to restore, maintain, or rebuild.

Back on NH 10, passing the Reeds Wildlife Management Area, you come into Orford, where there are opportunities for Connecticut River boating and fishing. Orford, thirty-four miles below your destination of Littleton, is a handsome town, with shops arranged along the left side of the road and fine Federal and Greek Revival homes on the "ridge" to the right. A bridge crosses the Connecticut River to nearby Fairlee, Vermont, and Lake Morey.

With Blackberry Hill and Cottonstone Mountain to the right, you continue your journey north past Cottonstone Farm and the Bickford Homestead, amidst a series of busy working farms. Go by Echo Hill, cross Bean Brook, and drive through the crossroads village of Piermont, where you go over NH 25C opposite Bradford, Vermont. Well east of the Connecticut River for a while, you travel to the Bedell Bridge Historic Site in Haverhill, where periodic views again emerge along the now meandering Connecticut River. A pretty park and boat access occupy the site of the former bridge.

Haverhill itself is a splendidly handsome village organized around two greens bordered by lovely, well-maintained Federal homes, a church, and civic buildings. Antiques dealers and bed-and-breakfast places are along the main road. From North Haverhill, with its fairground, the route drifts north past the Grafton County Complex and courthouse into the old mill and former railroad town of Woodsville, where you will find accommodations and motorist services. Local exploration northwest of town will lead you to another covered structure, the Bath-Haverhill Bridge.

Continuing upriver, you arrive shortly in nearby Bath on NH 10 and US 302. Take time to visit still another covered bridge over the tumbling Ammonoosuc River, behind the inviting general store and next to the Congregational Church, built in 1873. Bath was settled in 1766. This region was a place of rendezvous for Rogers's Rangers, who fled this way after attacking and destroying Saint Francis, Quebec, in skirmishes prior to the French and Indian Wars. Rogers's men missed their rendezvous with support troops; harried by pursuing Indians and beset by disease, many of the men died here along the river.

The road now follows a meandering intervale, runs through open pastures, and goes through junctions with Landaff and Mill Brook Roads. You'll pass a cluster of superb brick Federal houses as you drive through a slump (New Hampshire parlance for a dip or gully) and then proceed along the winding Ammonoosuc northeastward into Lisbon, a manufacturing town and home of New England Electric Wire. Good outlooks on the river continue as you approach

Littleton, a pleasant mountain community recently named one of the ten best small towns in America. You'll have a chance to sample the town's accommodations, restaurants, and shops as NH 10 and US 302 become West Main Street by the Beal House Inn in Littleton's attractive downtown section.

5

Route:

Plymouth and the Western Mountains

Highway:

Routes 3A, 25, 116, 112

Distance:

53.5 miles (one way)

An intimate look at mountains in the western lands of the White Mountain National Forest is the goal of this drive. The route begins just south of the major peaks in Franconia Notch, skirts them along the Baker River to the west, climbs through remote backwoods roads in tiny communities upstream, then works eastward on NH 112 around 4,800-foot Mount Moosilauke and 4,500-foot Mount Blue to North Woodstock via striking Kinsman Notch. An optional side trip through Franconia Notch is offered, too. Traffic is modest at the eastern end of this journey and almost nonexistent in the most rural, northwest sections.

The route begins at the junction of US 3 and NH 25 just north of the pleasant college town of Plymouth, accessed via Exit 26 of I-93 or by local roads. US 3 continues northward here, but you *go west* on NH 25 and NH 3A (the Tenney Mountain Highway) toward West Plymouth and Rumney. The route goes through a congested, built-up area, a tribute to mall ugliness in the heart of what is otherwise some of the most handsome hill country in the Northeast. Mount Pero, Beech Hill, and big Stinson Mountain lie to the right as you cross Clay Brook, which flows into the Baker River.

With fine views northwest, you go through the junction where NH 3A turns south to Tenney Mountain, but you *proceed ahead and west* on NH 25. Pass Polar Caves Park on the left and enter Rumney Depot, just east of Rattlesnake Mountain. The road pulls northwest, staying with the Baker River, on the right. The river can be accessed in West Rumney at the state-maintained rest area just beyond Halls Brook Road, nine and a half miles west of Plymouth. Pass the junction with NH 118 (see Drive 6, next chapter) and continue north opposite Plummer Ledge, with fine views of Upper Rattlesnake, Willoughby, and Carr Mountains to the right, or east. The road moves through some small farms and pastureland. You cross the wandering Baker River twice and come shortly to the Wentworth Town Hall on your right. To the right, off the main road, is the hidden little town green, almost a miniature, with its old church. The new town offices are just beyond.

There are several commercial campgrounds in this section of the journey. Views ahead to the imposing ridgeline of Mount Moosilauke begin to appear. One of the most prominent mountains on New Hampshire's western flanks, almost-5,000-foot Mount Moosilauke (pronounced *moos-a-lock-eee*), was formerly known to locals as Moose Hillock. Still others had known it as Mooseheeloc, probably closer to the original Indian title.

With Oak, Clifford, Peaked, and Clement Hills to the right, you come to the town of Warren, where you *continue north* on NH 25 as it crosses NH 25C (see Route #7, page 65) and pass Hildreth Dam,

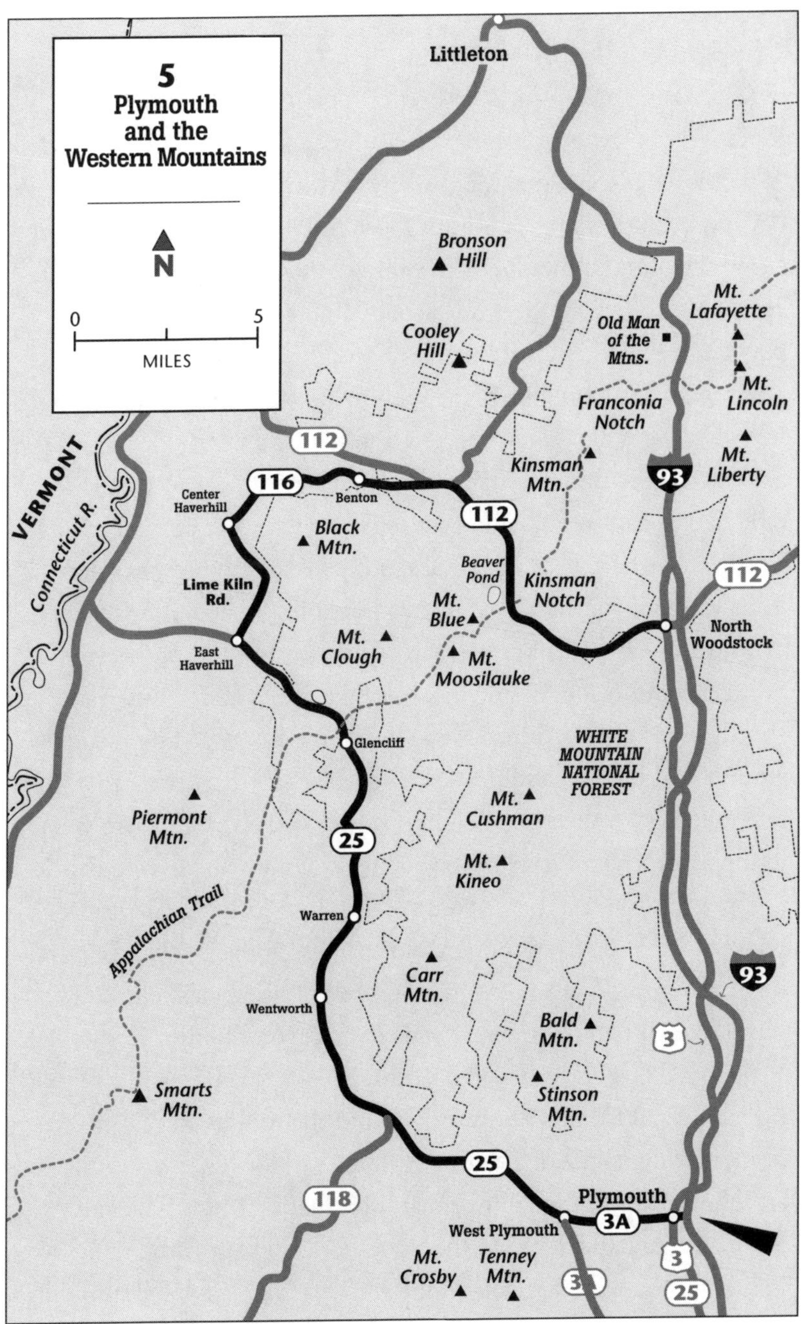
5
Plymouth and the Western Mountains
N
0
5
MILES
Littleton
Bronson Hill
Cooley Hill
Old Man of the Mtns.
Mt. Lafayette
Mt. Lincoln
Franconia Notch
Mt. Liberty
Kinsman Mtn.
VERMONT
Connecticut R.
112
116
Benton
112
93
Center Haverhill
Black Mtn.
Beaver Pond
Kinsman Notch
112
Lime Kiln Rd.
Mt. Blue
North Woodstock
East Haverhill
Mt. Clough
Mt. Moosilauke
Glencliff
WHITE MOUNTAIN NATIONAL FOREST
Mt. Cushman
Piermont Mtn.
25
Mt. Kineo
Appalachian Trail
Warren
Carr Mtn.
93
Wentworth
Bald Mtn.
3
Smarts Mtn.
Stinson Mtn.
25
118
Plymouth
West Plymouth
3A
Mt. Crosby
Tenney Mtn.
3
3A
25

which backs up the waters of Berry Brook. Old houses that are fine examples of New Hampshire vernacular architecture line the road as you leave town and climb northward toward Moosilauke and, beyond it, the summit of Mount Blue. Before long, you will skirt the east sides of those mountains. Coming into Glencliff, you enter Oliverian Notch, where the Appalachain Trail crosses the road. Just beyond, the bold cliffs of Blueberry Mountain loom over Oliverian Pond. Beyond to the north are open fields and working farms, where hay and clover are harvested in high summer.

After passing under a major power line, you come to East Haverhill, cross North Brook, and *bear immediately right* onto Lime Kiln Road. This sparsely settled rural road, which soon becomes dirt, leads through some high pasture (sometimes inhabited by flocks of wild turkeys) with fine eastward outlooks to the Hogsback and Sugarloaf and Black Mountains. For hikers, the Chippewa Trail shortly leads eastward from this road. Lime Kiln Road then curves around Knights Hill and descends sharply west-northwest to a point one mile east of the village church in Center Haverhill. Here you join NH 116 and *bear right* toward Benton and North Woodstock.

Going east on NH 116, you travel through forested countryside between Little Black Mountain and Whites Pinnacle toward Boutin Corner. The road meanders in a number of directions, climbs and dips through Benton, then ascends east. Beyond Boutin Corner, NH 116 joins NH 112 at the Wild Ammoonosuc River, where you *go right* on NH 112, drop eastward around the mountain massif you've been skirting, and enter Kinsman Notch. To the left are Mount Wolf and the three summits of Kinsman Mountain. Mount Blue and Mount Moosilauke loom to the right, above. Plan to stop at Beaver Pond and the Beaver Brook Trail for spectacular views up into the

The heart of Kinsman Notch: Mounts Moosilauke and Blue

bowl between these two impressive summits. This great granitic massif is the largest and most extensive of New Hampshire's western mountain groups. Its summit views extend far over Vermont and into eastern New York.

Kinsman Notch is famous for its winds. As they funnel northward from Woodstock and Lincoln, the gusts roar like surf, often presaging a storm. Fog sometimes runs up the valley ahead of the deteriorating weather; locals often used to say, "When fog runs up the mountains, rain runs down the hill." When the fog climbs the valleys hereabouts, some people will comment that "the devil is pumping fog out of Lincoln."

Pioneer Asa Kinsman opened up this valley. He had two sons, Lyman and Royal, who, while exploring the area one day, plunged deep into the ground. They had by accident discovered a series of caves that has been carved by the underground Moosilauke River.

In later days this territory and its submerged waters came to be known as Lost River.

Shortly beyond the Beaver Pond turnout, you will come to the Lost River Reservation as NH 112 dips southeast, then east, following Mount Moosilauke Brook to North Woodstock.

Once back in North Woodstock, you can make a side trip by following I-93 north through Franconia Notch. There are spectacular mountain views along I-93 in the fifteen miles north through the notch. Traffic congestion can be anticipated on summer weekends and in autumn as you approach Cannon Cliffs, the Old Man of the Mountains (New Hampshire's state symbol), and the Cannon Mountain Aerial Tramway. This side trip is best made during the week, especially at the height of the fall foliage season. Cannon Mountain, in season, is the site of an active alpine ski facility accessible from I-93.

6

Route:

Bristol–Mount Cardigan Loop

Highway:

Routes 104, US Route 4, Routes 118, 25, 3A

Distance:

56 miles

I can remember as a boy riding the train from White River Junction to Concord and seeing, far in the distance, the bold, cone-shaped profile of Mount Cardigan rising to the north. The great mountain seemed an isolated, lonely sentinel in the quiet woodlands of western New Hampshire. Those trains, alas, are now gone, but one can make an equally scenic drive around this 3,121-foot mountain today, returning along the western shore of popular Newfound Lake. The route also provides access to Mount Cardigan State Park and several attractive natural areas.

Begin this journey in the inviting west-central New Hampshire town of Bristol, on NH 104 about six miles west of I-93's Exit 23 in New Hampton. Once in Bristol, follow NH 104 (Pleasant Street) southwest out of town toward Danbury. Skirting Rowell and Merrill Hills in brushy countryside to the south, the route drops through Alexandria and crosses from Grafton County to Merrimack County.

You enter Elmwood and pass Searles Hill and the Danbury Bog Wildlife Management Area. This becomes heavily wooded, unspoiled country, broken only occasionally by settlements such as Danbury, where NH 104 and US 4 meet.

Continue westward now on US 4, proceeding through more hill country and a series of low summits too numerous to catalog. The road pulls more northwesterly in Grafton, continuing to Grafton Center with views ahead to prominent Isinglass Mountain. Side roads leave Grafton Center westward to the Grafton Pond Reservation, where there is access to fishing and boating. After passing Tewksbury Pond, you come shortly to Canaan, a small, bustling crossroads town with shopping and motorist services. Here you *leave US 4* and *head north* on NH 118 from the village center by the bandstand.

The Great Stone Dwelling at Shaker Village, Enfield

A brief side trip *west* via US 4 to Enfield will bring you to the old Shaker settlement and The Museum at Lower Shaker Village, on the *south* side of Mascoma Lake—very much worth a visit for those interested in the Shaker way of life and the superb craftsmanship of the Shaker tradition. Accommodations are available there in the Shaker-built Great Stone Dwelling, now an inn, on Route 4A in Enfield. (Highly recommended.)

On NH 118 you head through wild, unsettled territory along the Indian River and past Kimball Hill to Bucks Corner. The dramatic

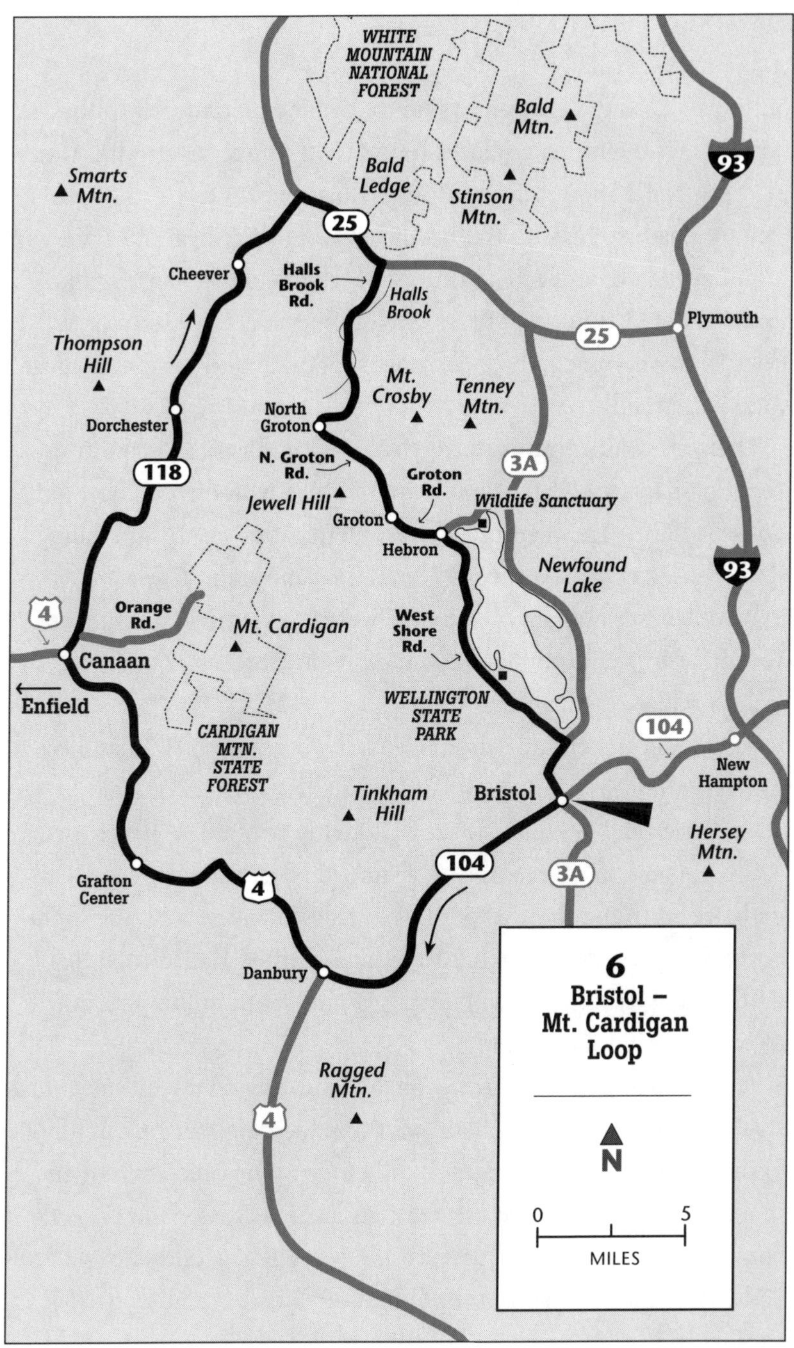
WHITE MOUNTAIN NATIONAL FOREST
Bald Mtn.
Smarts Mtn.
Bald Ledge
Stinson Mtn.
93
25
Cheever
Halls Brook Rd.
Halls Brook
Plymouth
Thompson Hill
Mt. Crosby
Tenney Mtn.
North Groton
Dorchester
N. Groton Rd.
Groton Rd.
3A
118
Jewell Hill
Groton
Wildlife Sanctuary
Hebron
Newfound Lake
4
Orange Rd.
Mt. Cardigan
West Shore Rd.
Canaan
Enfield
WELLINGTON STATE PARK
104
CARDIGAN MTN. STATE FOREST
New Hampton
Tinkham Hill
Bristol
Hersey Mtn.
104
3A
Grafton Center
4
Danbury
6
Bristol – Mt. Cardigan Loop
Ragged Mtn.
4
N
0
5
MILES

outline of Mount Cardigan, its long ridgeline tapering off to the north, is visible in many places to the right. Immediately after turning onto NH 118, watch for Orange Road, which leads to New Colony Road and east to trailheads for Mount Cardigan, in Cardigan Mountain State Forest. The trail network offers challenging hikes to the towered summit, with marvelous views over western New Hampshire. If you climb, wear proper footwear and carry extra gear, water, and food.

This side of Cardigan is mostly wooded, undisturbed country. You'll pass by deadwaters and scattered hills with only an occasional house or farm. The road imitates a roller coaster, rising and falling sharply as it makes its way to Dorchester and on to Cheever. Views toward Ames Mountain, north of Cheever, open up in an intervale. You drive by the diminutive town office in Dorchester, followed by a church that is equally tiny.

Just under fifteen miles from Canaan, you reach NH 25 and *bear right*, heading east. Fine views of Bald Ledge, Ames Mountain, and Currier Hill open to the west. Roughly two miles farther east, you will come to a State of New Hampshire rest area on your left with access to the shore of the lovely Baker River. About a mile beyond the rest area, watch for the well-marked Halls Brook Road on the right, where you will *bear right* and south in the direction of North Groton and Hebron.

Halls Brook Road climbs steeply and steadily on a winding course that will keep you busy. There is little traffic here, but be careful of approaching cars on the tight, blind curves. The brook is hidden in a ravine to the left, then to the right as it is crossed. You shortly come to a T intersection just past the Mary Baker Eddy house. (Eddy was the founder of the Church of Christ, Scientist.) *Go left and southeast* here on North Groton Road. The road makes a long, winding descent southeastward along Pine Brook to Spectacle Pond, with occasional fine views to the mountains ahead.

Reaching another **T** at Groton, you *bear left* toward Hebron on Groton Road. (If you go right at this junction, a brief drive west on Sculptured Rocks Road will bring you to the interesting natural rock formation of that name below Jewell Hill.)

Your route from Groton follows the Cockermouth River to Hebron, at the northwest corner of beautiful Newfound Lake. (A short side trip leftward along the north shore of the lake will bring you to Hebron Marsh Wildlife Sanctuary, to a trail with views down the lake, to another trail up Plymouth Mountain, and to the Paradise Point Nature Center in East Hebron.) Hebron itself is a fine collection of old buildings, a church, a village school, and a general store on an expansive green reminiscent of a New Hampshire that is fast disappearing. There is a wonderful unity to the architecture of this tranquil little settlement. Stopping by the green and resting for a moment to enjoy a quiet summer day brings a sure measure of contentment.

From Hebron, continue down the lake on West Shore Road. A lot of this stretch is heavily developed, perhaps inevitably, but there are open spaces where the water views are excellent. The route passes Owls Head, Nuttings Beach, and Hornet Cove. Wellington State Park is located here on the left. This attractive park provides shore access, fishing, hiking, swimming, and a picnic area.

Continuing south, watch for Fowler River Road on your right at a **T** intersection; a side trip on this road provides access to climbing trails and hiker accommodations on the east side of Cardigan Ridge. To continue the Bristol–Mount Cardigan Loop, at this **T**, you *stay* *left* on West Shore Road and follow it toward Bristol. You come eventually to a junction with NH 3A, which you join and travel *southward* to Bristol once again.

7

Route:

The Western Hills: North Woodstock to Piermont

Highway:

Routes 112, 118, 25, 25C

Distance:

32 miles (one way)

This route will take you through exceptional, unspoiled mountain country in the western precincts of the White Mountain National Forest (WMNF) and onward through attractive valleys and hills in rural western New Hampshire. Secluded mountain views open up, bold ledges are exposed, and hidden country lanes emerge in this drive on near-deserted roads beginning just minutes from a heavily traveled interstate.

Your journey departs from North Woodstock at Exit 32 on I-93. Come west into town to the junction of US 3 and NH 112. North Woodstock is a small mountain town, once a hikers' and rock-climbers' hangout, transformed by the tremendous surge of development and tourism locally and in nearby Lincoln, which had been a paper mill ghost town. Food, fuel, and accommodations are available locally. From North Woodstock, *go west on NH 112* toward Benton through a residential section, past the town offices, police station, and some campgrounds. Pass Russell Farm Road and follow Moosilauke Brook and Lost River west to the junction of NH 118, where you *bear left* toward Warren two and a half miles from Woodstock, escaping completely from I-93's congestion.

NH 118, the Sawyer Highway, enters the WMNF and climbs steadily to the south and west. There is that pleasant if surprised feeling of driving where there are suddenly no houses, no sign of human habitation. The deciduous cover common to the area makes this road and its surrounding hills brilliantly colorful come autumn. After passing Elbow Pond Road at five miles, you'll continue to climb to the west and northwest, getting up on the ridge in hardwood forest along a roadside dotted with wood ferns. The road climbs through heavily wooded country as it slabs across the Asquam Ridge of Mount Waternomee. Mountain views open up ahead periodically.

At seven and a half miles out, you reach a clearing and turnout on the left with spectacular views eastward to mountains of the Pemigewasset Wilderness along the Kancamagus Highway. Although the view is bounded, you get a sense here of the tremendous number of mountains clustered in this region of New Hampshire. Behind you, unseen, is the long ridge of Mount Moosilauke. From the height of land, NH 118 drops southwest and crosses the Warren town line, descending slowly past Ravine Lodge Road, with some fine views to the southwest. The drop steepens, with occasional mountain views on the right. Eleven miles along, you come to a cluster of houses and proceed west parallel to the Baker River, leaving the WMNF and entering the Baker River Valley. You'll pass the entrance to the old Moosilauke Carriage Road, now a hiking trail. Some pools appear in the river as you go past a campground at

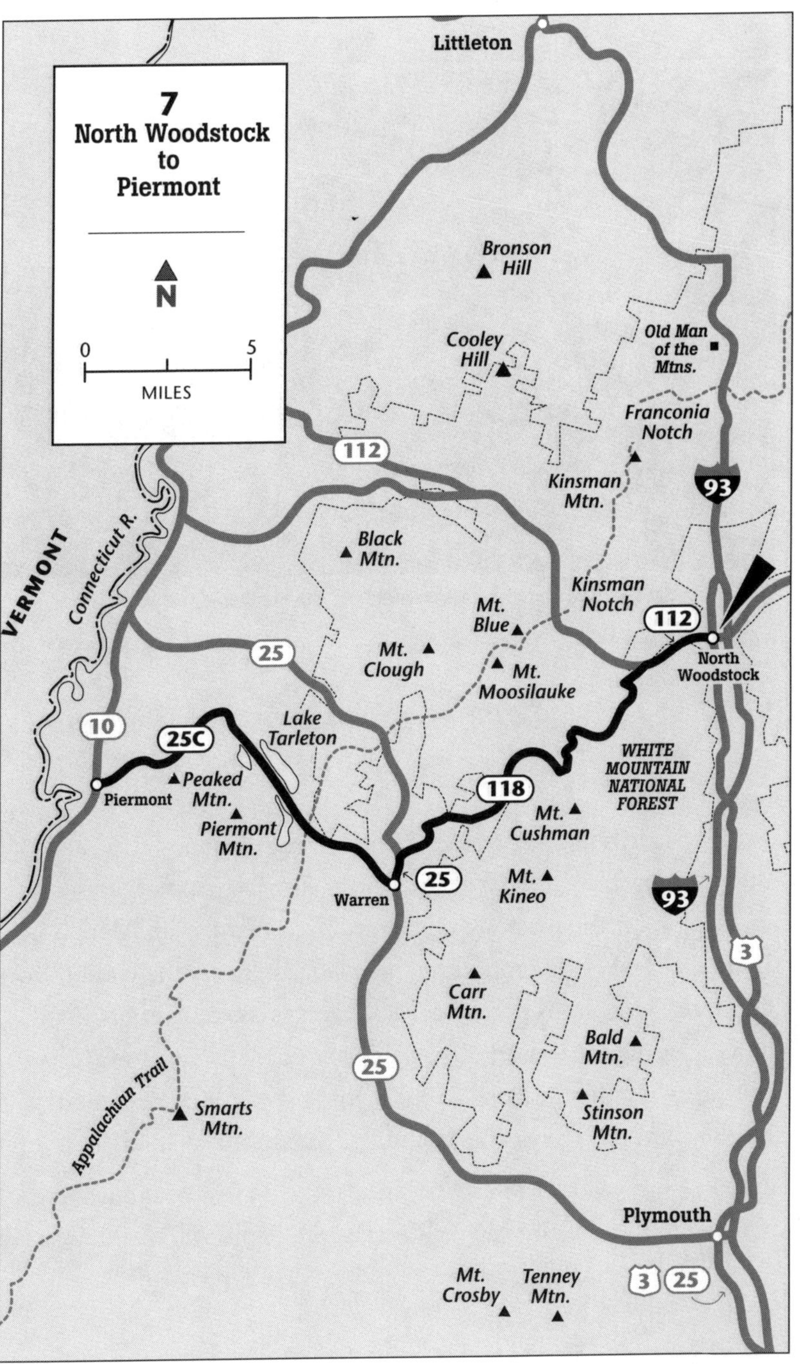
7
North Woodstock
to
Piermont
N
0
5
MILES
Littleton
Bronson
Hill
Cooley
Hill
Old Man
of the
Mtns.
Franconia
Notch
112
Kinsman
Mtn.
93
Black
Mtn.
VERMONT
Connecticut R.
Kinsman
Notch
Mt.
Blue
112
North
Woodstock
25
Mt.
Clough
Mt.
Moosilauke
10
25C
Lake
Tarleton
WHITE
MOUNTAIN
NATIONAL
FOREST
Piermont
Peaked
Mtn.
Piermont
Mtn.
118
Mt.
Cushman
Warren
25
Mt.
Kineo
93
3
Carr
Mtn.
Bald
Mtn.
25
Appalachian Trail
Smarts
Mtn.
Stinson
Mtn.
Plymouth
Mt.
Crosby
Tenney
Mtn.
3
25

Eastward to the distant mountains of the Pemigewasset Wilderness

Bachelor Brook Road and enter an intervale with mountain views southward. Shortly you arrive at a junction with NH 25 in the village of Warren.

Go left and south on NH 25 for barely a mile in a settled area, then *turn right* by the Warren Volunteer Fire Department and Common (look for the woefully uncharacteristic missile) on NH 25C. Immediately *go right* around the bandstand again at the end of the common, *heading north* now on 25C. After passing a lumberyard and emerging into broad farm fields with cattle, drive toward the ridges on the horizon. To the right and east are the emerging bold outlines of Hurricane Mountain, Mount Moosilauke, and Mount Blue.

The story is told here in Warren of a little girl, Sara Whitcher, who was left at home with her siblings one Sunday in June 1783, while her parents walked to a relative's house up the notch. On their return, Sara was missing, apparently lost while trying to follow her parents through the dense, roadless woods. A search was organized that went on for days, with no success. Sara was presumed dead. A clairvoyant, a fellow named Heath from Plymouth, told searchers that he could find her and knew that she was safe in the care of a bear near a brook. Searchers had, indeed, seen the tracks of a child and those of a large animal near a streambed. On following Heath's directions, the searchers found the girl alive and intact, if a bit hungry. She lived to tell her tale of the "big black dog" she remembered protecting her.

The road climbs abruptly northwestward for a while and comes to the Appalachian Trail, passes under a power line, and begins to descend again with mountain views ahead. This Glencliff region is strikingly attractive countryside. You will have noticed by now how refreshingly free of commercial development this entire route is.

The road crosses the Piermont town line twenty-one miles into this journey and heads due north along an open rib, with Lake Armington on the left behind a screen of trees. Lake Tarleton will be barely visible on the right and Lake Katherine is farther on the left. The road drops sharply now, crosses a brook, and curves westward through pasture down on the level once again. As you head away from the highest mountains, you still see low hills close in on both sides, and farms appear, some overgrown and going back to woods. Go around the unique, ledgy profile of Peaked Mountain to the left as you follow Eastman Brook. Pass Barton Bridge and go through a farmed intervale next, coming shortly to the junction of NH 25C and NH 10 in Piermont at the Four Corners General Store, where this journey ends.

8

Route:

Gorham: A Journey Through the High Peaks Region

Highway:

Route 16, US Routes 302 and 3

Distance:

58 miles (one way)

This route wends its way among the grandest peaks in New England. The loftiest summits in the northeastern United States are here, surrounded by lesser mountains, ravines, gulfs, and churning rivers fed by mountain runoff. It's dramatic country, always with something to engage the traveler's eye, and is a must-see experience for anyone visiting New Hampshire.

Begin this circuit of the high ranges in Gorham at the junction of NH 16 and US 2, by the Gorham Common. Gorham is a small, rapidly growing valley community at the bend of the Androscoggin River a few miles below Berlin. *Travel south* on NH 16 from Gorham, shortly passing the U.S. Forest Service ranger station, where White Mountain National Forest (WMNF) information and camping and fire permits may be obtained. You'll pass the starting points of the Carter-Moriah Trail and Stony Brook Trail on the left. The road momentarily crosses and follows the rock-strewn Peabody

River in this section. With Pine Mountain to your right, you begin to get glimpses of the higher summits ahead near Pinkham Notch.

In Martins Location you come to the WMNF's Dolly Copp Campground, a large, well-managed camping area where early arrival is advised to secure a campsite in high summer. The site is named after Dolly Copp, who—with her husband, Hayes—operated a hostelry here for more than forty years, beginning in the 1830s. Their place was the only shelter for those following the cart track that rose in the valleys southward and continued on to Randolph.

Local lore has it that in 1855, Nathaniel Copp of Pinkham's Grant was hereabouts on a four-day winter hunting trip. He took a large deer and dragged it home through the snow, then immediately returned to the woods to find another deer he had shot earlier. He was soon lost. Fearing for his life in the gathering darkness and thirty-below weather, Copp knew he'd better keep moving or he would surely freeze to death. He encountered and ran down another deer in the deep snow and killed it with his knife. He skinned the deer, then cut out its heart, which he put in his haversack for nourishment. He covered himself with the deerskin and continued to walk but became even more disoriented. He would not yield to his fatigue and kept on for hours. As the snowstorm gave way near noon the next day, Copp found himself in Gilead, Maine, near the mouth of the Wild River, forty miles from where he had started. He was discovered safe there by his friends still a day later, after they had followed his partially obscured tracks. His little adventure became known locally as "Copp's Walk."

Continuing southward on NH 16, you'll pass the Peabody Field site and the trail to the Imp Face just beyond. High to the left is the Carter-Moriah Range, with Mount Moriah, Imp Mountain, and

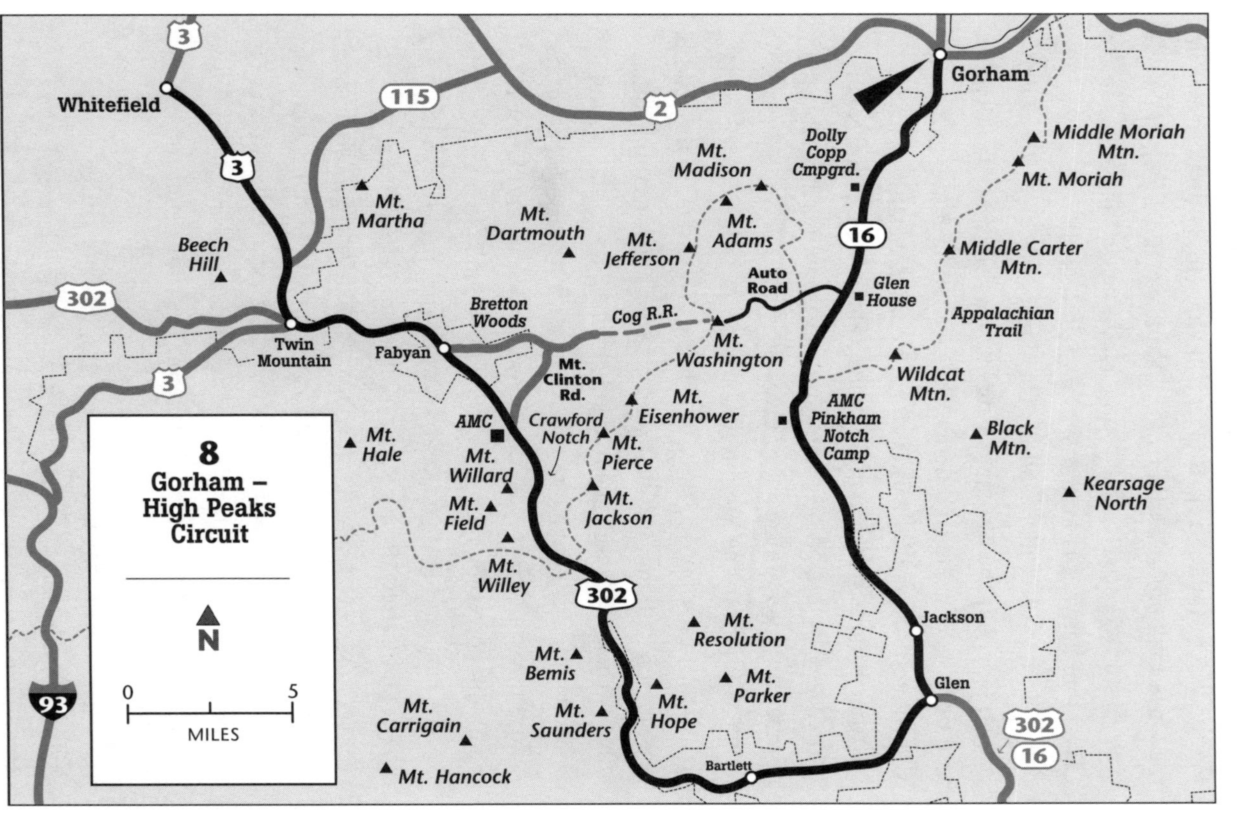
8
Gorham –
High Peaks
Circuit
N
0
5
MILES
Whitefield
Gorham
Twin
Mountain
Fabyan
Jackson
Glen
Bartlett
3
115
2
302
16
93
Beech
Hill
Mt.
Martha
Mt.
Dartmouth
Mt.
Jefferson
Mt.
Madison
Mt.
Adams
Dolly
Copp
Cmpgrd.
Middle Moriah
Mtn.
Mt. Moriah
Middle Carter
Mtn.
Glen
House
Auto
Road
Appalachian
Trail
Bretton
Woods
Cog R.R.
Mt.
Washington
Wildcat
Mtn.
Mt.
Clinton
Rd.
Mt.
Eisenhower
AMC
Pinkham
Notch
Camp
AMC
Crawford
Notch
Mt.
Pierce
Black
Mtn.
Mt.
Hale
Mt.
Willard
Mt.
Field
Mt.
Jackson
Kearsage
North
Mt.
Willey
Mt.
Resolution
Mt.
Bemis
Mt.
Parker
Mt.
Hope
Mt.
Saunders
Mt.
Carrigain
Mt. Hancock

North Carter Mountain periodically in view. To the right, views up the Great Gulf to the northern Presidentials gradually open up. Here, from right to left, are Mounts Madison, Adams, Jefferson, and Clay. More leftward is Mount Washington—as hikers say, "the big one"—at 6,288 feet in elevation. The Great Gulf, a perfect glacial cirque, separates the Mount Washington massif from the other summits. Sited at the confluence of Canadian air currents, Mount Washington boasts the world's worst recorded weather, with an instrument-measured maximum wind velocity of 231 miles per hour. Many have died on the mountain's upper reaches, and the number is added to nearly every year.

The entrance to the Mount Washington Auto Road appears on your right now, opposite the Glen House. The drive up the road to Washington's summit can be made for a fee but is recommended only for those with well-maintained vehicles, good brakes, and a penchant for driving along precipices with thousand-foot drops.

Traveling on NH 16 past the Wildcat Ski Area and Wildcat Mountain, you come momentarily to Pinkham Notch Camp, hub of the Appalachian Mountain Club's (AMC) trail network in the Presidential and Carter-Moriah Ranges. Pinkham Notch Camp is worth a visit for information about the region. Camp-style meals are served here, and overnight accommodations of a rustic sort are available. There are also several pretty, undemanding local walks around Pinkham in addition to the tough routes that head north and west into the ravines. Inquire at the information desk for details of local nonalpine hikes.

NH 16 now drops rapidly to Jackson, a pretty village with a variety of accommodations at any time of year and home of a vast network of cross-country ski trails in winter. There are sleigh rides here

In the heart of the high peaks region

in snow season beneath Thorn Mountain. Jackson is also the site of nationally sanctioned Nordic ski races and a well-preserved covered bridge over the Ellis River.

Just below Jackson, you enter the often busy crossroads of Glen, then *bear right* at the junction of NH 16 and US 302 and head west. Follow 302 by Bartlett Bridge and through Cooks Crossing, next passing Attitash Ski Area. You soon come into tiny Bartlett, at the junction of Bear Notch Road and US 302. This is the last community before you enter Crawford Notch. After passing Sawyer Rock, the road bends northward and follows the banks of the lovely Saco River, where there is good fly-fishing. After passing through Harts Location, usually one of the first communities in the nation to vote in presidential elections, you head north, with high mountains hemming in both sides of the road. Mount Hope and

Bemis Ridge are to the right, and Mount Saunders and Mount Bemis are to the left. The trailhead for Nancy Pond, back in the Pemigewasset Wilderness, lies to the left also.

Farther along, you'll spot the Davis Path, which ascends rugged Montalban Ridge, then climb toward the Willey House site, opposite Frankenstein Cliff. The first road through this notch was built in 1803, and for years the primitive route was devoid of any habitation, an inconvenience for the many carters who moved loads along this turnpike, headed for Portland. Henry Hill opened a shelter in 1823; two years later, it was taken over by the Willey family, who gradually improved the place.

In August 1826, bad weather followed a drought. Cattle were driven from the intervales in anticipation of floods. A major mountain storm arrived, touching off a landslide that swept away all seven members of the Willey family and two servants, burying them alive. They had taken refuge in an outbuilding, thinking themselves safe. The roaring landslide missed their usual sleeping quarters but killed them all in the outbuilding.

If you look up carefully to the northwest, you will see, opposite, the railroad tracks that traverse the famous Frankenstein Trestle. Summer rail excursion services from North Conway have been resumed here in recent years. The sheer, dramatic, forbidding Webster Cliffs are above to the right of the notch as you skirt Mount Willard (left) and ascend steeply to the head of the notch. The road levels off, and ahead is Crawford Notch railway station, a superb example of New England railway architecture, now preserved and run as an information center by the AMC.

Just beyond the railway station is an AMC-operated overnight shelter, across the road from the junction of the Avalon Trail and

Crawford Path. On the right-hand side of US 302 is Mount Clinton Road, which leads to the Mount Washington Cog Railway, a century-and-a-half-old steam railroad that climbs the north side of the great mountain on a regular summer schedule.

Crawford Notch takes its name from the illustrious Crawford family who first settled this windswept region. Ethan Allen Crawford was born in 1792 in a log hut at the head of the notch at an Indian burial mound known as Giant's Grave. In 1819 he and his father, Abel Crawford, cut the first path along the southern Presidential Range. Ethan is also believed to have built the first stone shelter on Mount Washington's summit. Nearly seven feet tall, he seemed impervious to the cold and sometimes walked barefoot in the snow without coat or hat. Like those of his father before him, Ethan's exploits in the mountains became legendary. He captured bear cubs often and tamed them, wrestled with big bears who had become caught in his traps, and battled wildcats into submission. He did not go to health clubs.

Heading northwest, US 302 now drops rapidly toward Bretton Woods and Fabyan, site of the famous Mount Washington Hotel. It is a grand classical edifice reminiscent of resort life in these mountains a century ago, when "sports" would arrive on the trains from eastern cities to spend weeks or often the whole summer in the mountain air. There are striking views of the entire Presidential Range from here, an uninterrupted series of high peaks once known as the Crystal Hills.

That name originated when explorer Darby Field, the first white man to climb to the summit of Mount Washington, discovered samples there of what he called "Moscovy glass," probably quartzite, which he thought might be diamonds or have similar value. By

1672, the name White Mountains was in use, perhaps derived from the name used by the Algonquin Indians, which meant "white rocks." Early mariners often observed these hills from well out at sea, noting a band of distant white summits nearly lost in the clouds about a hundred miles away. Local indians called Mount Washington *Agiochochook*, and the whole Presidential Range *Waumbek-Methna*, or "mountains with snowy foreheads." The pretty watercourse that drains the northern Presidentials was known as *Singrawoc* and is today known as the Israel River.

From Fabyan, US 302 roams west along the banks of the tumbling Ammonoosuc River, which has its headwaters between Mounts Washington and Monroe, toward the little community of Twin Mountain. Peaks of the Dartmouth Range lie to the northeast as you travel, and Mounts Deception and Dartmouth are most prominent. From Twin Mountain, you now *turn right and northwest* on US 3 and follow this road through high plateaulike lands to the village of Whitefield, surrounded by a halo of low mountains, with great, open views ahead to Vermont.

9

Route:

Wolfeboro and the Sandwich Range

Highway:

Routes 109, 113, 113A

Distance:

37 miles (one way)

The country east of Lake Winnipesaukee and north to the Sandwich Mountains is quintessential New Hampshire. Great inland waters give way to splendid uplands, then to bold mountains. Beautiful at any time of year, this region of the Granite State basks in a certain glory in the foliage season, when its winding back roads are surrounded by thousands of acres of dense color. This route, which begins in the attractive lakeshore village of Wolfeboro, makes its way along some of Winnipesaukee's notable bays, runs northward to picture-book towns in the Sandwich Mountains, then heads east to the tiny crossroads of Tamworth.

Wolfeboro is a long-established lakeside colony, home of Brewster Academy and host to the Wright Museum of American Enterprise. Sitting atop Wolfeboro and Back Bays and the outlet for the waters of Crescent Lake and Lake Wentworth, the town is a pleasant collection of old houses, inns, restaurants, and shops, busy in summer

Lakes border the mountains on many New Hampshire scenic routes.

and quieter in winter but always thoroughly welcoming. Across Wolfeboro Bay are enticing views of the Belknap Mountains over Lake Winnipesaukee.

This trip begins on North Main Street, NH 109, which becomes Ossipee Mountain Road as it heads northwest toward Winter Harbor and Tuftonboro Neck. You shortly pass the Libby Museum, then go by Mirror Lake to the right and Winter Harbor to the left and turn north through Tuftonboro. There are numerous outlooks southwest across twenty-mile-long Lake Winnipesaukee, and plenty of boat liveries and launching facilities. You arrive shortly at a junction with NH 109A at Melvin Bay. Here you'll have more fine views across the bay to Moultonborough Neck.

Beyond Melvin Village, just up the road from Melvin Bay, you'll see periodic water views to the left as you drive through Clark Landing and to another junction, this time with NH 171. Faraway Mountain, Black Snout Mountain, and the Larcom summits of the Ossipee Mountains lie eastward. *Continue northwest and left here,*

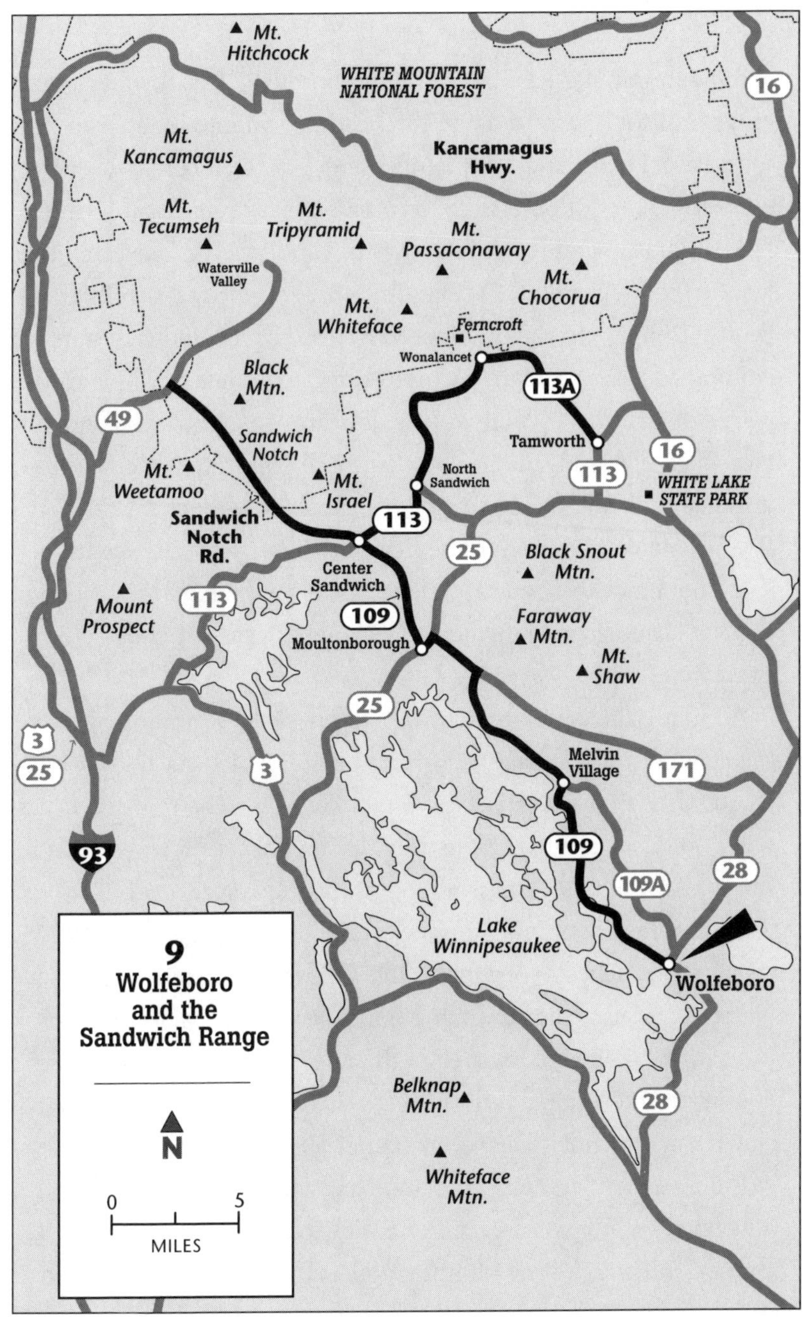

Mt. Hitchcock
WHITE MOUNTAIN NATIONAL FOREST
16
Mt. Kancamagus
Kancamagus Hwy.
Mt. Tecumseh
Mt. Tripyramid
Mt. Passaconaway
Waterville Valley
Mt. Chocorua
Mt. Whiteface
Ferncroft
Wonalancet
113A
Black Mtn.
49
Sandwich Notch
Tamworth
16
Mt. Weetamoo
Mt. Israel
North Sandwich
113
WHITE LAKE STATE PARK
Sandwich Notch Rd.
113
25
Black Snout Mtn.
Center Sandwich
113
Mount Prospect
109
Faraway Mtn.
Moultonborough
Mt. Shaw
25
3
25
3
Melvin Village
171
109
93
109A
28
Lake Winnipesaukee
Wolfeboro
9
Wolfeboro and the Sandwich Range
N
0
5
MILES
Belknap Mtn.
28
Whiteface Mtn.

coming in minutes into busy Moultonborough. This town is a major crossroads for motor traffic in the bustling summer months and on foliage weekends in late September and early October.

Go left and west on NH 25, *then take an immediate right* to stay on NH 109 northward toward Sandwich. You leave the lakes country for the mountains now. Outstanding views to the major hills above Sandwich open up as you proceed northward to Sandwich in rolling countryside along a high, pastured ridge. Continue north, and soon a long descent from Wentworth Hill brings you around a bend and past the fairgrounds into Center Sandwich, a lovely village of predominantly white-painted homes in classic New England rural style. If you time your autumn drive here just right, you can take in the small but enjoyable Sandwich Fair, usually early in October. League of New Hampshire Craftsmen and Ayotte's Designery shops are located here, too.

An interesting side trip is possible from here, beginning opposite the general store on Sandwich Notch Road, which travels northwest through the hills to NH 49 in Waterville Valley. The route becomes gravel surfaced as it wends its way through beautiful woodlands in the White Mountain National Forest. This low-speed, primitive road is kindest to vehicles with high clearance, good brakes, and firm suspensions. Check your fuel gauge before setting out. Sandwich Notch Road also leads to hiking trails over Mount Israel and to trails in the Guinea Pond area of the notch. This side route enters country of exceptional beauty. If you drive through it, please do so slowly and carefully, leaving no sign of your passing.

From Center Sandwich, continue east and northeast on NH 113, a wooded country road to North Sandwich, with Mount Israel, Guinea Hill, and Young Mountain off to the left in the Sandwich

Range. From North Sandwich, you plunge further into mountain country *on NH 113A, going north* through Whiteface, then working your way east to Wonalancet. Here, the Ferncroft site is the hub of dozens of trails that lead to the summits of major mountains, such as Whiteface, Passaconaway, Hibbard, Paugus, and Wonalancet.

Wonalancet was, many years ago, the center of efforts to breed a hardy sled dog for arctic work. A successful breed evolved that came to be called Chinook. The winters in this vast mountain valley were an excellent testing ground, and dogsledding was and is a regular winter sport here. As you skirt the hills, to the northeast is Mount Chocorua, New Hampshire's "little Matterhorn," its peaked, ledgy summit a favorite destination of hikers and a much photographed subject for travelers. Driving farther southeast on NH 113A, you pass through pretty Hemenway State Forest and, in a few minutes, conclude this trip in the little crossroads village of Tamworth.

Several choices exist for travel beyond this point. A few miles east of Tamworth is heavily traveled NH 16 for journeying north or south. North lie the major summits of the White Mountains, the Kancamagus Highway, and roads leading to the western mountains of Maine. (See the author's *Maine's Most Scenic Roads*, Down East Books.) Just southward on NH 113 is NH 25, a link to central New Hampshire and the Lakes Region to the west. White Lake State Park, on NH 16, is only a short drive east. The park has more than two hundred tent sites as well as showers, canoe rentals, a camp store, and waterside hiking trails.

10

Route:

Gorham: A Northern White Mountains Loop

Highway:

US Route 2, local roads, Routes 110, 110B, 16

Distance:

56 miles

This journey takes travelers around the less-visited northerly peaks of the White Mountain National Forest. It is a long loop, with a return via the banks of the Androscoggin River north of Berlin, and offers outstanding mountain views from numerous points along the way. The high alpine country seen from this trip is as spectacular in winter as in other seasons and makes an inviting drive during the fall foliage months; the leaves turn earlier here in the cold mountain air.

Your trip begins in Gorham, at the bend of the Androscoggin where the river gallops east and heads for Maine. At the junction of NH 16 and US 2, *head west* from Gorham on Route 2 toward Jefferson. The route climbs steadily on a long rise, passing the entrance to Moose Brook State Park (camping) and entering the little intermountain town of Randolph. On your left are Pine Mountain, then Howker Ridge, which rises to the summits of Mounts Madison and

Adams. These 5,000-foot-plus peaks are the northern tail of the massive Presidential Range and are reached via a well-marked network of trails from the left side of the road. The *Airline Trail*, which you will pass, ascends Durand Ridge to the Appalachian Mountain Club's Madison Hut. (Hiking in this region requires extra clothing, mountaineering boots, and stamina suitable to traversing rough, steep terrain.) This and other trails depart to the summits from a parking area known as Appalachia.

US 2 wends its way farther westward, with the summits of the Crescent Range to the right and opposite Appalachia as you travel toward Bowman. You'll soon pass Valley Road on the left as US 2 bears northwestward, and there are expansive views of Mount Washington and the southern Presidentials over the lower hills of the Dartmouth Range to your left. Mount Washington, at 6,288 feet, and the peaks around it represent the highest sustained ridgeline in the northeastern United States. The summits of Washington, Monroe, Franklin, Eisenhower, and Clinton are visible trailing toward the southwest. The scene is breathtaking. In minutes you come to the crossroads of Jefferson beneath Mounts Starr King and Waumbek in the Pliny Range, with fine views southwestward toward the Pondicherry Wildlife Refuge and the Cherry Mountain Range.

From Jefferson, *take a right* on North Road and go northwest toward Grange. This secondary road crosses Elm Ridge just east of Lancaster, where you *bear right and north* on Grange Road in hill country and shortly pass through the tiny hamlet of Grange itself. From Jefferson to this point, you have been making a gradual turn around the northwest end of the Pliny Range, with its distinctive three summits: Mount Pliny, Mount Waumbek, and Mount Starr King. Beyond Grange, this road passes through the equally lonely

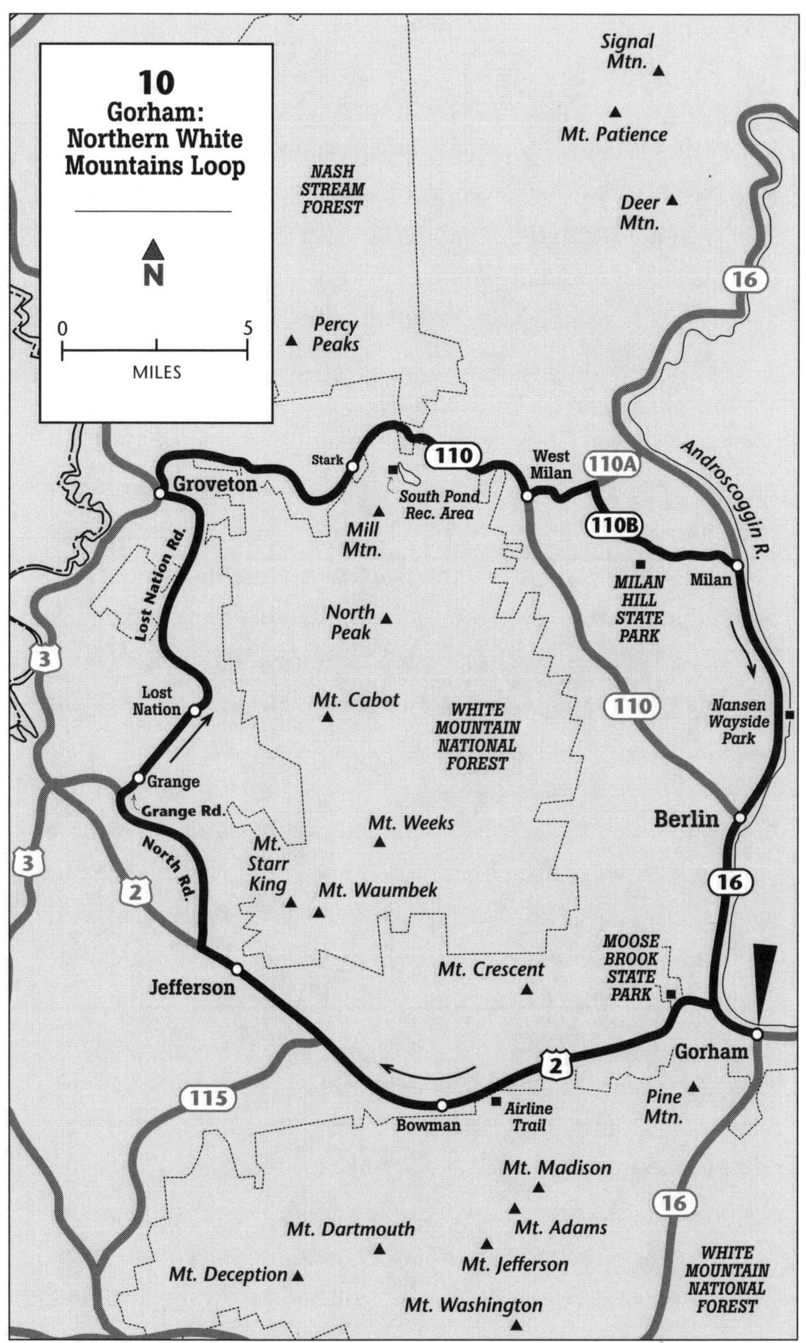

10
Gorham:
Northern White
Mountains Loop
N
0
5
MILES
Signal Mtn.
Mt. Patience
NASH STREAM FOREST
Deer Mtn.
16
Percy Peaks
Stark
110
West Milan
110A
Groveton
South Pond Rec. Area
Mill Mtn.
110B
Androscoggin R.
Lost Nation Rd.
MILAN HILL STATE PARK
Milan
North Peak
3
Mt. Cabot
WHITE MOUNTAIN NATIONAL FOREST
110
Lost Nation
Nansen Wayside Park
Grange
Grange Rd.
Berlin
Mt. Weeks
Mt. Starr King
North Rd.
3
2
Mt. Waumbek
16
MOOSE BROOK STATE PARK
Mt. Crescent
Jefferson
Gorham
2
115
Pine Mtn.
Bowman
Airline Trail
Mt. Madison
16
Mt. Adams
Mt. Dartmouth
Mt. Jefferson
WHITE MOUNTAIN NATIONAL FOREST
Mt. Deception
Mt. Washington

settlement known as Lost Nation, from which this section of the route takes its name. Views eastward to looming Mount Cabot, Hutchins Mountain, and other summits in the remote Pilot Range appear from time to time in majestic relief on the horizon to your right. Lost Nation Road soon bends westward and ends in the border town of Groveton, where accommodations and other traveler services are available.

From Groveton, take NH 110 (the Stark Scenic and Cultural Byway) east in rolling woodlands to the village of Stark at Stark Bridge. To Stark's southeast rises 2,500-foot Mill Mountain. Victor Head and Bald Mountain lie to the north. You continue through Percy toward Milan on NH 110, with views into the dense cluster of hills southward. Several miles beyond on the right, in largely unsettled countryside, watch for a road leading to the South Pond Recreation Area and to trails for the Devils Hopyard and Kilkenny Ridge. Hikers will find trails here that follow Cold Stream to North Peak and Rogers Ledge.

This remote country is much tied to logging and has few of the comforts of cities. In such remote corners, rural New Hampshire people once tended toward superstition. Famous American writer William Dean Howells, a regular visitor to New Hampshire's north country, noted that when country folk in these parts saw a multitude of things go wrong, day after day, and believed themselves victimized by some hidden force, they would say, "the witch is in it." New Hampshire poet Robert Frost carried the notion of rural spirits still further in his extended verse *The Witch of Coos*.

Forsaking superstition, you pass Location Hill to the south. NH 110 next goes through a series of bends and reaches West Milan at its junction with NH 110A. *Go left* here and follow this byroad for a

Northern White Mountains near Randolph

few miles to its junction with NH 110B, where you then *turn southeast* and *right* over Jodrie Hill to Milan. Watch for the entrance here to Milan Hill State Park, where a short auto road takes you to superb views all the way north to Canada, to the Presidential Range, and into Maine.

From Milan, this roving mountain journey *bears right, or south*, on NH 16 along the scenic, free-flowing Androscoggin River. As a local story relates, Mettallak, son of the chief of the Coosuc Indians, once lived here on the banks of the river. He eventually became leader of his tribe and was well respected for his fearlessness. Still, bad times came as "civilization" encroached, and his tribe disintegrated. His children moved to the settler's towns, then his wife perished. Mettallak placed her body in a canoe and headed down the Androscoggin to a deserted island, since named for him. He buried his wife there and lived in solitude by her grave for many years. In 1846, he was discovered almost blind and near starvation and was rescued.

Continue south on NH 16, passing Nansen Wayside Park, site of the old Nansen Ski and Outing Club jump, one of the great pioneering ski and snowshoe venues in North America. Although Berlin is thought of as predominantly a Franco-American community, there is some evidence of Norwegian settlement in the area, too, and thus the Nordic influence represented by the Nansen tradition. Dropping farther south on NH 16, you wend your way through the busy streets of Berlin, a city of great paper mills. Staying on NH 16, you continue southward through a built-up area to your starting point in nearby Gorham.

11

Route:

A Northwestern Circuit: Littleton to Twin Mountain

Highway:

Route 135, local roads, US Route 2,
Roues 115A, 115, US Route 3

Distance:

40 miles (one way)

An interesting journey can be made in New Hampshire's northwestern hill country above and east of Littleton. This territory lies adjacent to Vermont's Northeast Kingdom and shares the sparsely settled, mountainous remoteness usually associated with that cold, beautiful region. The area also contains two New Hampshire state parks and a private memorial woodland.

Set out westward from Littleton, a pleasant border community on the Ammonoosuc River served by I-93, US 302, and NH 10, 18, 135, and 116. From the Beal House Inn on West Main Street, *take NH 135* toward North Littleton and Gilman. *Keep right* at a fork where NH 18 goes left and NH 135 bears northward and reaches the Connecticut River close to Cow Brook in North Littleton. Continue northeast and you'll soon cross Carpenter Brook, west of picturesque Towns Mountain, Mount Misery, and Blue Hill.

As you approach Cushman, watch for Harriman Road on the

right, where you can gain access to the Ruth and Slade Gorton Memorial Forest on Beede Mountain. Beyond Cushman, your journey continues northeast through Dalton, and you *stay north* on NH 135 at its junction with NH 142 by the Connecticut River opposite South Lunenberg, Vermont. Excellent views of the river continue as you reach Mount Orne Bridge, then work your way eastward as NH 135 arrives in Lancaster, just north of Orne Mountain and Mount Pleasant. A worthy side trip may be made from Lancaster to Weeks State Park, just two miles south of town on US 3, which here is named the Prospect Mountain Road Scenic and Cultural Byway. Once an intermountain crossroads, present-day Lancaster has a pleasant, traditional main street and a variety of services. Inquire locally for directions to the three nearby covered bridges.

In the Lancaster area, an old story is told of a young woman named Nancy who worked for Colonel Whipple in Jefferson. The girl fell in love with another servant. She allowed him to hold her money and her heart, assuming that he would soon marry her. While she was in Lancaster preparing for the wedding, she learned that the man had left without her, and she rushed back twelve miles to Jefferson to pursue him. Though exhausted, she followed his tracks through deep snow into the roadless woods for another ten miles beyond Jefferson. She was later found frozen to death, sitting upright against a tree. In Crawford Notch, Nancy Brook and Nancy Hill have been given her name. Her former lover, hearing of what he had inflicted on this poor young woman, went mad and died within months in an asylum.

From the Lancaster fire station and police headquarters, at the south end of Main Street, *go east* on Mechanic Street, through a covered bridge, and join Middle Street at Weeks Medical Center. Fine

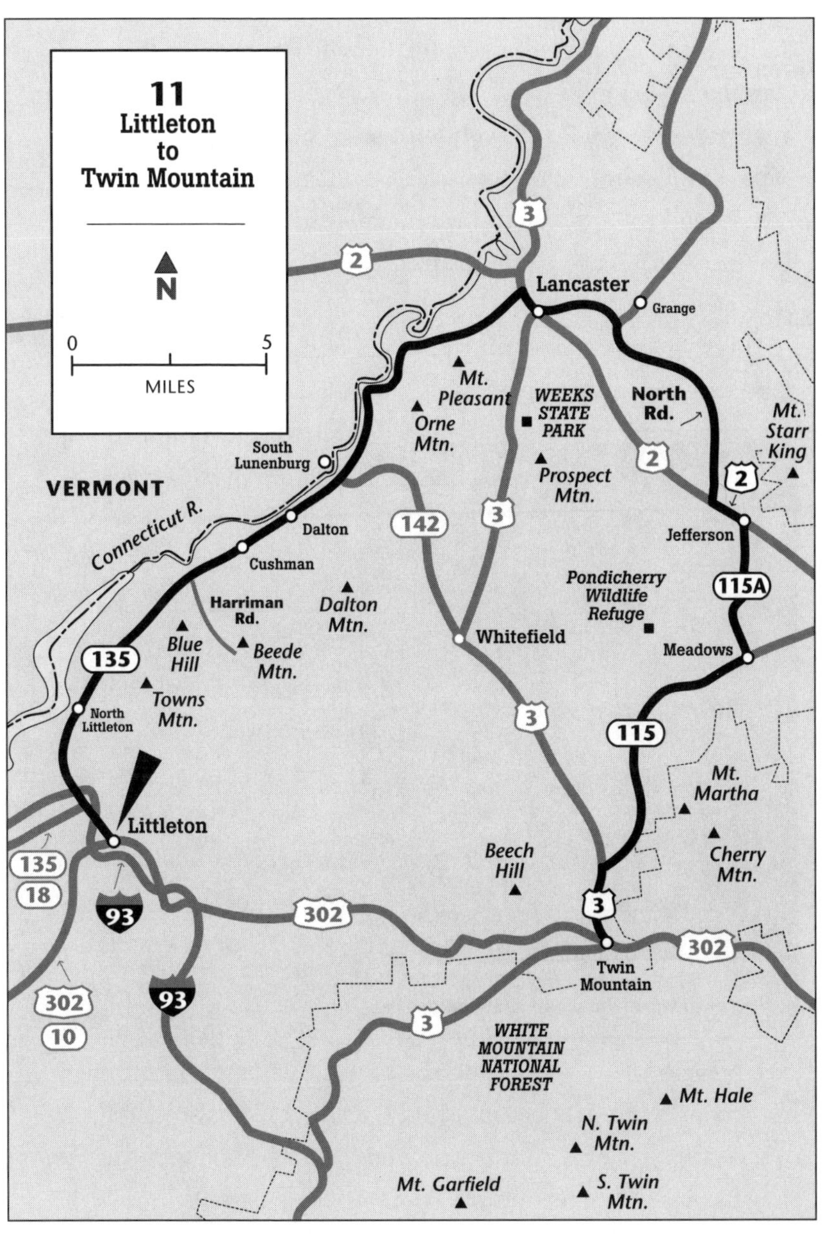

11
Littleton
to
Twin Mountain
N
0
5
MILES
VERMONT
Connecticut R.
South Lunenburg
Dalton
Cushman
Harriman Rd.
Blue Hill
Beede Mtn.
Dalton Mtn.
Towns Mtn.
North Littleton
Littleton
135
18
302
10
93
302
3
2
Lancaster
Grange
Mt. Pleasant
Orne Mtn.
WEEKS STATE PARK
Prospect Mtn.
North Rd.
Mt. Starr King
2
Jefferson
142
Whitefield
Pondicherry Wildlife Refuge
115A
Meadows
115
Mt. Martha
Cherry Mtn.
Beech Hill
Twin Mountain
WHITE MOUNTAIN NATIONAL FOREST
Mt. Hale
N. Twin Mtn.
S. Twin Mtn.
Mt. Garfield

outlooks to the major peaks of the Pliny Range open up here and continue ahead most of the way. In fact, you shortly travel along an intervale on North Road, with horizon-to-horizon views of mountains. Pass Grange Road two miles from Lancaster, go over Otter Brook, and roll through farm country with sheep in the pastures. The massive hulk of Mount Starr King is directly ahead as you proceed along North Road.

This route proceeds through a series of rural crossroads, bearing southeast and away from Grange toward Jefferson. (Certain rural crossroads have had a special place in northern courtships, often being the scene in days past of what were called shift marriages. A woman, often widowed, appeared in only her shift at night at a carefully chosen county crossroads to be married. Standing exactly at the point of intersection of the crossroads, she was in no county and all counties at once, thus blurring jurisdiction. Nearly naked in only her shift, she brought no liens or encumbrances with her. Her groom could thus marry her without any fear of incurring her or her former husband's debts. Such were the cunning tactical solutions of rural hill life in these parts.)

Small, western New Hampshire towns maintain a traditional feeling.

Keep right at the junction of Gore Road and North Road, pass a campground on your right, and arrive at the junction of US 2 in Jefferson. *Bear left and east* on US 2, which you follow just a few hundred yards before bearing right on NH 115A. Follow this road south to its junction with NH 115 at Meadows. You are just east of the Pondicherry Wildlife Refuge and in a cluster of imposing, dramatic mountains that rise all around you. The Dartmouth Range lies just to the southeast. Mount Martha, Owls Head, and The Humps rise to the south in the attractive Cherry Mountain Range. Go right and southwest on NH 115, skirting this range, and pass the Cherry Mountain trailhead on your left near Carter Brook.

The summer of 1885 in this region was marked first by cold, wet weather and scattered violent thunderstorms. After a period of very warm weather, the storms returned in July. On Friday, July 10, a landslide started at Owls Head and built momentum and volume as it raced down the mountain. The broad swath of the tumbling slide just missed the Boudreau farm but swept away Oscar Stanley's barn, from which he and three workmen fled seconds before impact. One of Stanley's cows lost a horn to the slide and was badly bruised, but it survived. Donald Walker, buried and rescued, survived his ordeal but died a few days later on his projected wedding date. Tourists swarmed over the area to witness the destruction and to be photographed with the one-horned cow. The place soon had a carnival atmosphere, with food and drink being sold, and the sheriff's men were summoned to close down the rum sellers.

This drive concludes in the midst of mountain country by descending southwest to the junction of NH 115 and US 3, where you continue southward on US 3 to Twin Mountain, a small upland community that backs up to the White Mountain National Forest and Garfield Ridge.

From Twin Mountain, travelers may proceed west on US 3 to Franconia Notch or southeast on US 302 to Crawford Notch (see Route #10, page 85). There are traveler accommodations and motorist services on this route in Littleton, Lancaster, Jefferson, Whitefield, and Twin Mountain.

12

Route:

Durham–Pawtuckaway Loop

Highway:

Routes 155, 152, 156, 107, 43, and local roads

Distance:

42.5 miles

Durham is the site of the University of New Hampshire, a large, public, land-grant institution lodged in rolling countryside near the Oyster River about four miles southwest of Dover and the Spaulding Turnpike (NH 16) and eight miles from Portsmouth. Durham is a pretty campus town and worth a tour on foot, which offers an opportunity to see various university buildings, several academic schools and departments, the Dimond Library, and the Paul Arts Center, all radiating outward from steepled Thompson Hall, on the rise in midcampus. There are attractive Georgian-style dormitories on Main Street, the pleasant Victorian-cum-Italianate architecture of "T Hall," the plain red brick of several older classroom buildings such as James Hall, a Greek Revival gem in colonnaded Hamilton Smith Hall, and a host of industrial-modern buildings in the university's expanding science areas.

Durham is also your stepping-off point for a short loop drive westward on rural roads to Pawtuckaway State Park and back again. From opposite Thompson Hall, follow Durham's Main Street northwest just a mile, then *bear left* and *west* on NH 155A toward Lee. This road winds through attractive fields and woods, soon crossing the Oyster River at its junction with Chelsey Brook. You shortly join NH 155 (Mast Road) and follow it southwest to the center of Lee, a tiny village clustered around a small common. Bennett and Lee Hook Roads intersect NH 155 here.

Drive south through uncongested rural countryside, crossing Little River and Beaver Brook, until NH 155 reaches NH 152 at Kirkwood Corners, where you *bear right* and *west*, heading for South Lee. Stay on NH 152 as it crosses NH 125 in South Lee, just under eight miles from Durham, and continue west, crossing the North River and passing Vienna Smith State Forest and the General Bartlett Memorial Forest. There are several old farms here marked by silos, barns, and open pasture on hillsides. Isinglass Hill lies south and to your left as you come in minutes into the village of Nottingham, where NH 152 joins NH 156. Here, eleven and a half miles from Durham, you *go sharply left* onto NH 156.

You now begin a long loop around the 5,500 acres of Pawtuckaway State Park, a multipurpose woodland with seasonal opportunities for swimming, camping, canoeing, picnicking, fishing, snowmobiling, and cross-country skiing. You drift southwest past a church and go through Nottingham Square on NH 156. A cluster of pretty older homes lines the road south of here. Soon, to the right at Seamans Point, there are limited views of Pawtuckaway Lake. Cross the Raymond town line fifteen miles into this drive. About two miles beyond this point, on the right, watch for Harriman Hill and Mountain Roads, which provide entry to fishing,

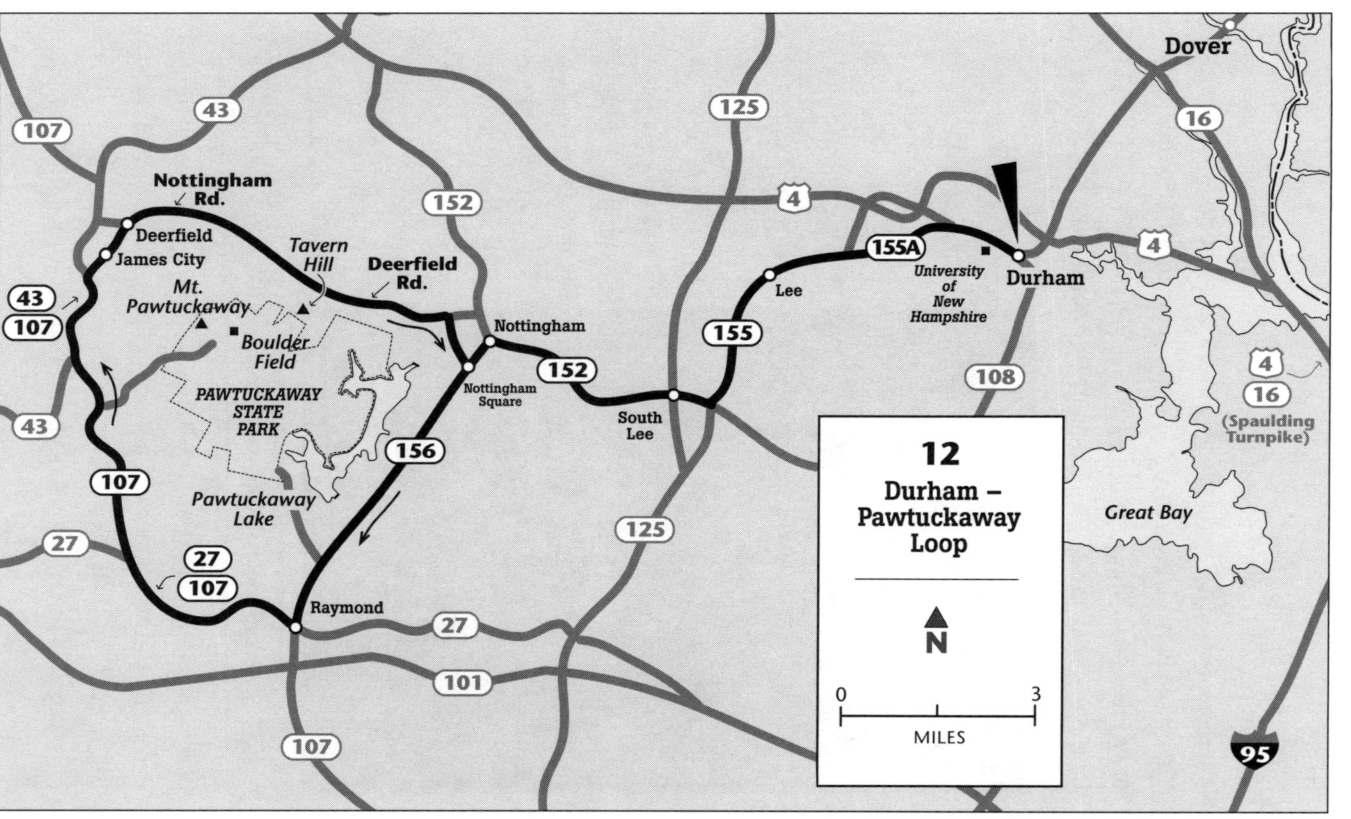
12
Durham –
Pawtuckaway
Loop
N
0
3
MILES
Dover
Durham
University of New Hampshire
Lee
South Lee
Nottingham
Nottingham Square
Deerfield Rd.
Tavern Hill
Nottingham Rd.
Deerfield
James City
Mt. Pawtuckaway
Boulder Field
PAWTUCKAWAY STATE PARK
Pawtuckaway Lake
Raymond
Great Bay
(Spaulding Turnpike)
4
16
155A
155
152
156
125
108
43
107
27
101
95

swimming, and camping areas on the southeast side of Pawtuckaway State Park on Pawtuckaway Lake. The entrance is well marked.

Past the park access road, you come momentarily to the junction of NH 156 with NH 27 and NH 107 in Raymond. *Go right* and *west* here on NH 107 and NH 27 to skirt Raymond Center along the banks of the Lamprey River. This is a wide, busy, developed section of road. Rounding Long Hill and crossing Dudley Brook, you follow northwest along the Lamprey, then continue on NH 107 as it leaves NH 27. Passing Norway and Robinson Hills on the right, NH 107 continues northwest along the western edge of Pawtuckaway State Park.

Busy streams make their way through rock cuts in New Hampshire backcountry.

Watch for Reservation Road on your right if you want to make a side trip into the center of Pawtuckaway State Park. Follow Reservation Road to Mountain Road, circle Pawtuckaway Mountain to the left (north), and descend to the Boulder Field. Near Round Pond, the Boulder Field is an interesting area of enormous, glaciated rocks dumped here during the retreat of the glacial ice sheet more than eleven thousand years ago.

Back on NH 107, proceed north and shortly *keep right* on NH 43, riding it almost into Deerfield Center. Then, *go right* along Deerfield Parade Road, a side road in the James City section. You are now eighteen miles from Durham.

From Deerfield and its tiny green, follow Nottingham Road and Deerfield Road *right* and *east* through sparsely settled rural terrain along the north side of Pawtuckaway State Park. The road travels by many fine old houses and farms and some high-walled pasture, then becomes more wooded again. There are occasional views south toward Pawtuckaway Mountain. This countryside is quite wild and rich in game. (I recall, years ago, researching a magazine article here. I spent days accompanying a New Hampshire Fish and Game wildlife biologist on a meandering trek as we used radiotelemetry to follow a collared black bear. Little beeps from the radio receiver were often our only clues as we tracked the secretive bear through these snowy woods.)

Beyond Tavern Hill, which lies to your right, Deerfield Road crosses Back Creek and Mill Brook. Thirty-three miles out, as the road winds east, you come to a launch site for boats on Pawtuckaway Lake. The short side trip to the channel is worth making. The road then drops east above Pawtuckaway Lake. Occasional openings in the dense forest reveal flooded bogs, before the road begins climbing to its junction with NH 156 at Nottingham Square. Go *left* on 156 and north to its junction with NH 152 in Nottingham. This completes the long, pretty loop around Pawtuckaway State Park. Here you *turn right* and *east* on NH 152 and retrace your earlier route through Lee back to Durham.

Note: Exploration of Pawtuckaway State Park is a must on this journey. There are ample facilities here in pretty woodlands for swimming and picnicking, and there are 193 campsites, a playing field, a camp store, and canoe and paddleboat rentals. Tel. (603) 895-3031.

13

Route:

A Seacoast Ride: Portsmouth to Exeter

Highway:

Routes 1B, 1A, 111

Distance:

22.5 miles (one way)

One gets a deepened sense of New Hampshire's history in the old towns of the seacoast region. Here are buildings, gardens, and scenes dating back to New Hampshire's earliest days as a growing royal colony. As in much of New England, the coastal zone became the starting place for early communities, government, education, and trade. The Portsmouth-Exeter region bears the full stamp of colonial life amidst modern-day amenities.

This journey takes you between two popular historic seacoast communities via the Atlantic shore, with opportunities to walk about and explore in what can become a fine day trip. We begin in Portsmouth at New Hampshire's riverine border with Maine. Portsmouth is New Hampshire's active seaport, an attractive small city on the Piscataqua River that has seen rapid growth in recent years. Dating to the early 1600s, Portsmouth's Strawbery Banke was the scene of colonial settlement and is today the site of a working community museum open to the public. In addition, many fine houses may be found in the city's riverfront area, some of them built from wealth garnered in early trade with the West Indies. A walk around the city's old section is highly recommended. Areas close to the riverfront have been refurbished in recent years, and small shops and restaurants occupy the harborside buildings.

Literary figures such as Thomas Bailey Aldrich, editor of the *Atlantic Monthly* and a leading American poet, grew up here. James T. Fields, of Boston's prominent Ticknor & Fields publishing company, was born in Portsmouth, and Celia Thaxter, author of highly valued accounts of life on the Isles of Shoals, was also from here. Thaxter's father was an innkeeper of great repute on these islands.

The harbor is a busy one for both pleasure craft and large ships that come upriver to industries in Portsmouth and nearby Newington. Across the river lies the Portsmouth Naval Shipyard, the U.S. Navy's main repair and refitting facility for nuclear submarines.

Good places to start examining Portsmouth's older sections on foot are the waterfront area on Market Street, Ceres Street, Court Street, and the lanes around Prescott Park. Market Square is architecturally interesting, and the Portsmouth Athenaeum is a real gem. Many restored period houses reside in Strawbery Banke, off Court Street. This section of the city is also home to a number of excellent restaurants and several appealing bed-and-breakfast establishments. (There are additional attractions just across the Piscataqua on the Maine side of the river. See the author's *Maine's Most Scenic Roads* and *Walking the Maine Coast*.)

From Prescott Park on the riverfront in Portsmouth, *follow NH 1B* (New Castle Avenue) east to the island village of New Castle, founded in 1693. On narrow streets you'll find old Fort Consti-

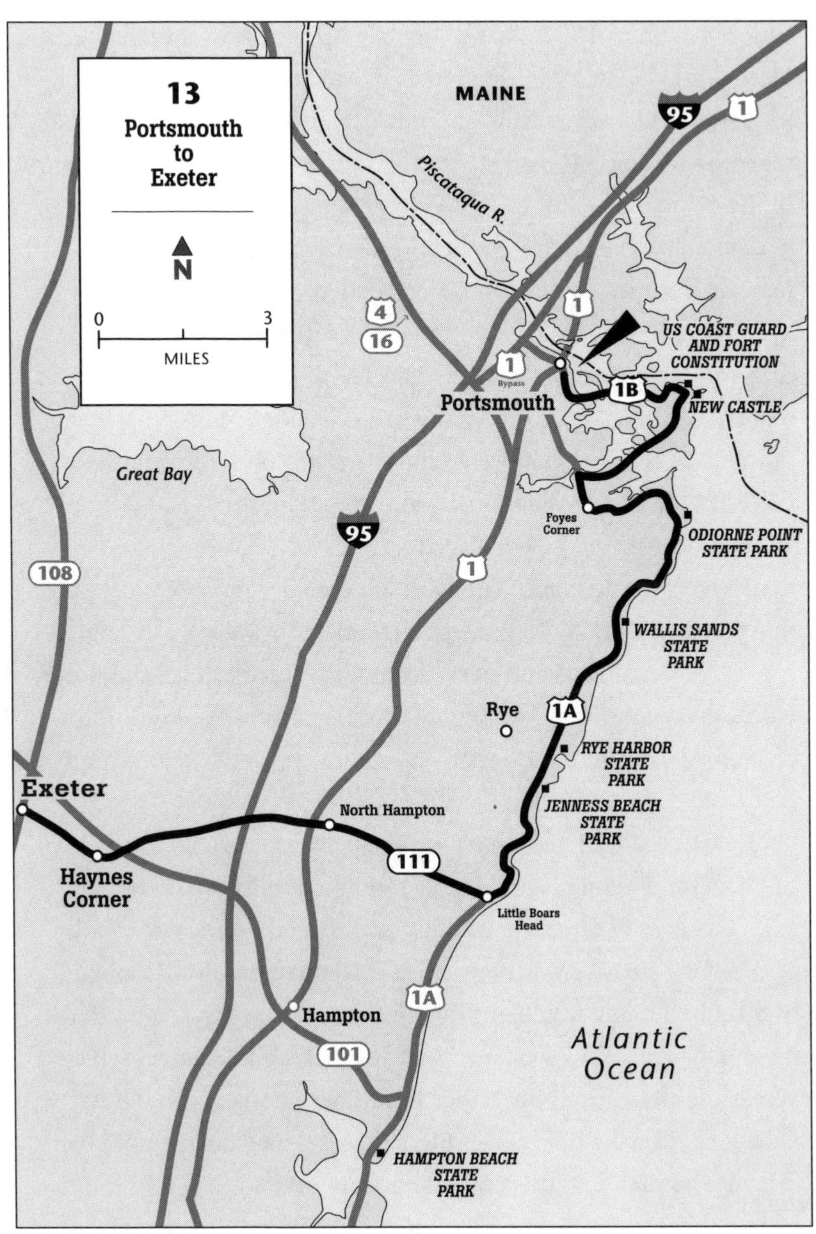

13
Portsmouth
to
Exeter
N
0
3
MILES
MAINE
95
1
Piscataqua R.
4
16
1
US COAST GUARD
AND FORT
CONSTITUTION
1
Bypass
1B
Portsmouth
NEW CASTLE
Great Bay
Foyes
Corner
95
ODIORNE POINT
STATE PARK
108
1
WALLIS SANDS
STATE
PARK
Rye
1A
RYE HARBOR
STATE
PARK
Exeter
JENNESS BEACH
STATE
PARK
North Hampton
Haynes
Corner
111
Little Boars
Head
1A
Hampton
Atlantic
Ocean
101
HAMPTON BEACH
STATE
PARK

tution, begun in 1632, next to the U.S. Coast Guard installation and New Castle Light, established in 1771. In anticipation of the British sequestering its armaments and powder, the fort was stormed and taken by revolutionaries early in the uprising against English control of the colonies.

Continuing south on 1B, you come shortly to Great Island Common on your left, a beautiful, tree-shaded park with views to Whaleback Light and beyond to the Isles of Shoals. The road next drops to Little Harbor and joins NH 1A, where you *bear left* and *south*. Nearby on 1A is the Wentworth-Coolidge Mansion, a splendid relic of colonial grandee architecture and once the family seat of Governor Benning Wentworth and the clan he sired. *Stay left* on 1A at Foyes Corner as the road pulls northeastward through a fine marsh to Odiorne Point State Park. One often sees hawks cruising this marsh, especially in winter. Some pleasant walking through oceanside woodlands and over old military fortifications can provide a diversion here. A variety of flowers, shrubs, and bird life enlivens the grounds, and there are salty views and breezes north and east.

Continue south on 1A to Rye, with superb water views to the Isles of Shoals and White Island Light, prominent offshore to the southeast. The Isles of Shoals have their own legends going back to the 1600s. One story recalls how a visitor to the isles was disturbed to find himself being watched through the window of a fishing shack by an ethereal young woman. He heard her wild laughter ripple across the stones, and his glance found her young and beautiful, with long, flowing hair. Suddenly, she was gone. Later, an old fisherman who had seen this apparition from time to time told the visitor about the woman. What the visitor did not know was that this fair spirit, even then, had been seen at the shoals for more than a hundred years. Believed to be the ghostly wife of Captain Scot, a pirate associate of Bluebeard, she had taken on the eternal task of guarding the treasure that Scot had hidden all over these islands until her long-deceased husband should come to claim it and her. To those who dared speak to her, she stared fixedly at the sea and said only, "Someday he shall return." Rumors of buried treasure persist. The isles may be reached by motor packet daily from Portsmouth Harbor.

Seaward outlooks continue as you drive past Wallis Sands and Concord Point, soon reaching Foss Beach and attractive little Rye Harbor. Farther on, you may wish to pause at Jenness Beach State Park before driving farther south to Little Boars Head, where you *turn right* and *west* on NH 111 toward North Hampton. This road takes you past many fine older houses and gardens as you approach North Hampton, cross US 1, and continue west to Exeter.

Driving through the Hamptons reminds one of the tale of Gen. Jonathan Moulton. In colonial times, the general was well known in this area for his bravery, military prowess, and hard bargaining. He had set himself up well in coastal Hampton but was nonetheless dissatisfied with his substantial success. Put simply, he wished to become the wealthiest man in the colony, bar none. He summoned the devil flippantly with an oath and was astonished when that creature at once appeared in his sitting room, dressed in black velvet. Moulton agreed to sign away his soul, and the devil promised to fill the general's boots with gold guineas on the first of each month.

Still not content, the ever-greedy general thought that he would have the best of the transaction and cheat the devil. He carefully cut the bottoms off the boots, so the more the devil filled them with gold coins, the more the boots emptied, until Moulton's chamber was waist deep in gold pieces. For months, the devil poured gold into Moulton's bottomless boots, until one day he discovered that the general was cheating him. That night, Moulton's house mysteriously burned to the ground, and with it the hidden guineas, which the general had secreted in the walls and above the rafters of the building. After the fire, Moulton searched the ruins for months but found no trace of his riches. Not long after his death, Moulton's coffin was exhumed and, when opened, found to be empty.

First settled in 1638, Exeter is a fine old academy town, New Hampshire's third major coastal community after Portsmouth and Dover. The Reverend John Wheelwright, a brother-in-law of Massachusetts Bay Colony dissenter Anne Hutchinson, obtained a deed to area lands from the Squamscott tribe and organized the first church here. Exeter residents were of a nonconformist bent and fought payment of taxes to the royal government, offering "a red-hot spit and a scalding" to any government agent bent on collecting the king's taxes in Exeter.

The famous Mast Tree Riot of 1734 occurred here when colonials, dressed as Indians, dragged London's agents from their beds when the crown attempted to restrict cutting of the best trees for the Royal Navy. For a time the fledgling New Hampshire legislature met in Exeter. Today, the town is dominated by Phillips Exeter Academy, which was established by wealthy merchant John Phillips in 1783. He also founded Phillips Andover Academy in Massachusetts and was a supporter of Dartmouth College. Phillips Exeter Academy is a center for education and the arts. In the town center, the League of

New Hampshire Craftsmen maintains a shop displaying the excellent work of New Hampshire artisans. A stroll around the town introduces you to many handsome old houses and the academy grounds at the confluence of the Exeter, Little, and Squamscott Rivers.

14

Route:

Through Border Country: Rochester to Conway

Highway:

Routes 125, 153

Distance:

53.5 miles (one way)

A very appealing journey can be made to the White Mountains along the web of back roads that straddles New Hampshire's rural border with Maine. From Rochester, the Lilac City, to Conway, at the mouth of the Kancamagus Highway, these roads wind through little hamlets and wander along numerous lakes. At their northern end, the roads reach the foothills of the great White Mountains. Of equal advantage, these back roads get you north without having to go the distance on often crowded NH 16.

This trip commences in southeastern New Hampshire, just north of Dover and Portsmouth. Rochester, first settled in 1728, is a small manufacturing city on the banks of the Cocheco River. It grew from the kernel of seacoast commerce begun in Portsmouth and Dover in the late 1600s. Captain Timothy Roberts led the settlement of this area and was followed in 1744 by the Reverend Amos Main, who took to preaching here. East Rochester is traversed by the Salmon

Falls River, a source of waterpower significant in the region's growth.

Indian raids kept Rochester on the verge of extinction in its earliest days and held the settlement to small numbers for at least two decades. Commerce eventually blossomed, however, and sawmills, gristmills, tanneries, and farming fed the colonial economy. Woolen mills later became a main feature of Rochester manufacturing. A jumping-off place for enterprise to the north, the Lilac City was later the hub of four regional railroads. Writer Sarah Orne Jewett used Rochester as the setting for her novel *Deephaven*. Present-day Rochester has a variety of motorist services, accommodations, and restaurants.

From Rochester, *take NH 125* (Wakefield Street) *north* through a built-up area along the Salmon Falls River to North Rochester and Milton. You soon come to rural country. Cross Great Brook, then go through the center of Milton and pass Milton Pond, to the right. The road climbs Milton Ridge shortly, and you come to the New Hampshire Farm Museum on the left. This innovative retrospective on traditional New Hampshire farm life provides demonstrations of blacksmithing, shoemaking, and other typical farm arts, keeping alive agricultural skills and structures once common in the Granite State. The museum is composed of an interesting assemblage of typical New Hampshire farm buildings.

At Laskey Corner, *keep left* on NH 125 and continue north through the tiny village of Union, with its cluster of homes reminiscent of many nineteenth-century, rural New Hampshire towns. The old train depot still stands here, a mute reminder of how these places were once connected by rail. At Union, NH 125 joins NH 153, which you *follow north* along Union Meadows and Pike Brook to Sanbornville, on Lovell Lake. The route now runs north-

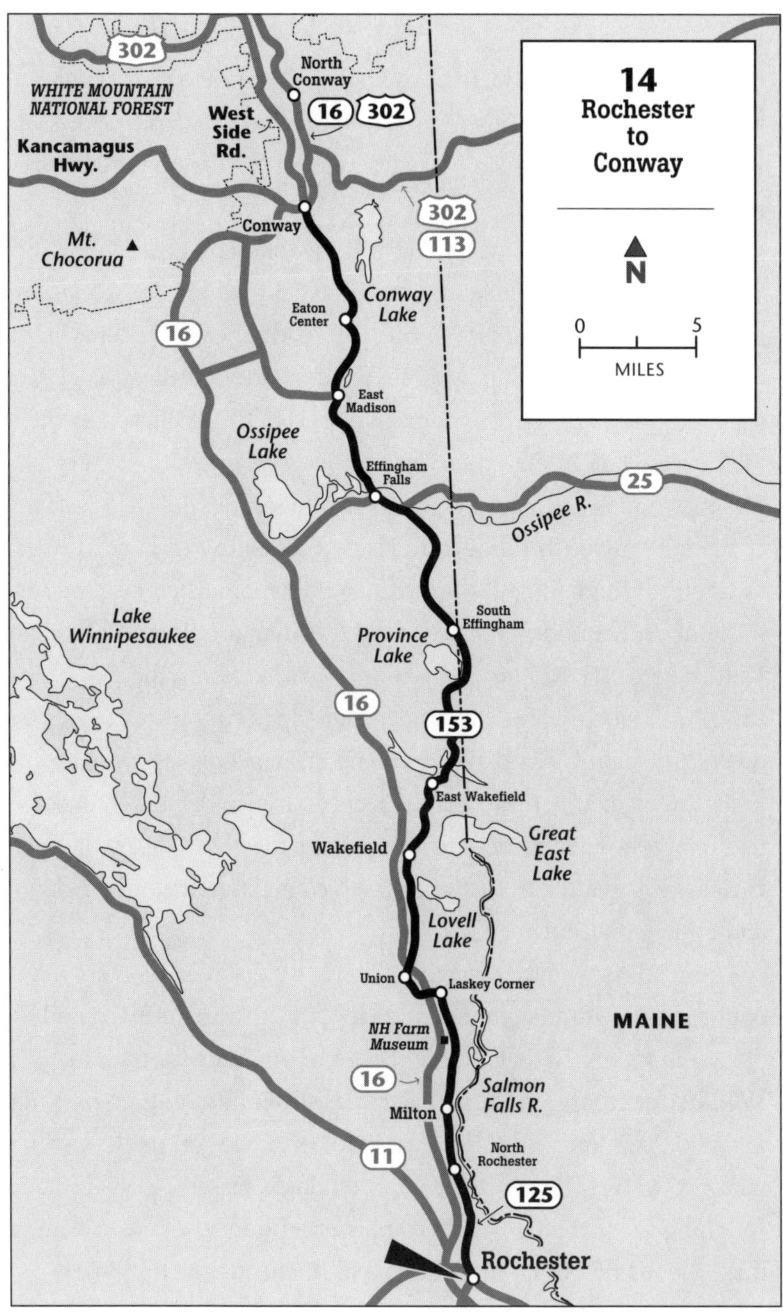

302
WHITE MOUNTAIN NATIONAL FOREST
North Conway
16
302
West Side Rd.
Kancamagus Hwy.
14
Rochester to Conway
N
0
5
MILES
Conway
302
113
Mt. Chocorua
Conway Lake
Eaton Center
16
East Madison
Ossipee Lake
Effingham Falls
25
Ossipee R.
Lake Winnipesaukee
South Effingham
Province Lake
16
153
East Wakefield
Great East Lake
Wakefield
Lovell Lake
Union
Laskey Corner
MAINE
NH Farm Museum
16
Salmon Falls R.
Milton
11
North Rochester
125
Rochester

east in increasingly attractive wooded countryside and through architecturally interesting Wakefield village. You soon pass Canal Road, on the right, which provides boating and fishing access to nearby Great East Lake.

You meander *northeast* on NH 153 in woodlands bisected by Scribner and Copp Brooks to East Wakefield, where you go around the south end of Pine River Pond. The road dips east to Sand Pond and Woodman, then climbs along the east side of Belleau Lake to the crossroads village of Province Lake. NH 153 pulls across the Maine state line briefly; then, back in New Hampshire, it runs by Province Lake's east shore, with good outlooks across the south end of the lake to South Effingham. Here your route heads northwest to Center Effingham and northeast to Effingham, then *heads northwest* once more and joins NH 25 for less than a mile into Effingham Falls, where NH 153 *turns northward* again, crossing the Ossipee River. Occasional views of Ossipee Lake open to the west. The now quiet Effinghams once basked in commercial success. A complex of mills constructed here along the Ossipee River in the 1820s once tied the economies of these several villages together. That earlier prosperity is still evident in the well-preserved architecture of Effingham and Effingham Center.

The road rises northward toward East Madison as it enters hill country, with gradually emerging views northwest to Blazo and Stacy Mountains, Goe Hill, and Bald Ledge. You pass the Hoyt Wildlife Sanctuary on Purity Lake in East Madison and go by King Pine Ski Area. As a side trip, East Madison Road, on the left, will take you to NH 113 and Madison Boulder, a massive glacial erratic weighing more than a hundred thousand pounds, deposited in these woods by glacial movement and fracturing. NH 153 next wanders along the west bank of Long Pond, Hatch Pond, and Crystal Lake, then heads into Eaton Center. Here NH 153 turns east for a short distance, then quickly northwest between Rockhouse and Atkinson Mountains. You then proceed along Page Randall Brook for nearly five miles to the town of Conway and the junction with busy NH 16 in the heart of the Eastern Slopes.

From this point, there are a number of choices for further travel. From NH 16 just west of the town center, the famous Kancamagus Highway (NH 112) heads west through the undeveloped Pemigewasset Wilderness to New Hampshire's western mountains. Although this road may see substantial traffic in high summer and foliage season, it is a truly exceptional drive and highly recommended. It will also connect you with several excellent excursions in western New Hampshire (Routes #5, #6, and #7, described on pages 53, 59, and 65).

In summer, autumn, and ski season, it is essential to avoid North Conway and its honky-tonk congestion on NH 16. During foliage season, on summer weekends, and on some ski-season weekends, it can take well over an hour to get through town. You can go around North Conway by using West Side Road from Conway to US 302 in Glen, thus connecting with other mountain-region drives in this book (see Routes #8 and #10, pages 71 and 85). From Conway you can also take NH 113 eastward to the beautiful Evans Notch region of Maine.

15

Route:

Claremont to Keene

Highway:

Route 12

Distance:

40 miles (one way)

Southwestern New Hampshire's border with Vermont, about as far from the madding crowd as one can get, provides a fine drive south in Connecticut River country. This route—sometimes inland, sometimes right by the river—provides an introduction to an area of New Hampshire not heavily visited yet abundantly rich in attractive sights. Additionally, this route offers that most appealing of benefits, the opportunity to tour scenic hill country without contending with heavy traffic. As a fall foliage trip, this drive especially beckons.

Set out from Claremont, a welcoming community in western New Hampshire situated roughly twenty miles below Hanover. Claremont, one of New Hampshire's largest towns, was first settled in 1762. Along with Lebanon and Keene, it is a major commercial center in the Connecticut River region. It straddles the Sugar River, a tributary of the Connecticut, and lies in the shadows of Green and Barber Mountains, which look westward to Vermont.

Travelers will want to stop in Tremont Square, the hub of this bustling community, near the site of the old town hall, built in 1896. This steepled brownstone, an imposing Victorian eminence, looks southward over the green. Colonel Benjamin Tyler built a dam on the Sugar River in 1764 and later constructed a gristmill in Claremont, an early effort to capture vital waterpower in the territory. The river is still visible on the north side of the business center. Asa Meacham established woolen mills here in 1813, and other mills and smelters followed. The town became a cotton milling center after the construction of looms in 1831, and papermaking also developed as a major industry. Historically, the town has been the site of an elaborate annual Russian Easter celebration. Inventor Albert Ball, developer of the Springfield repeating rifle, was born and raised here. There are varied accommodations, restaurants, and motorist services in the area.

The imposing tower of Claremont's City Hall

Drive southwest from the center of Claremont on NH 11 and 12 (Pleasant Street) and past Moody Park. After going through a commercial section, you quickly enter less built-up countryside, run alongside Calavant Mountain, and pass Unity Stage Road in North Charlestown. NH 11 and 12 pull gradually closer to the Connecticut River now, with Hubbard Hill State Forest to the left at the base of

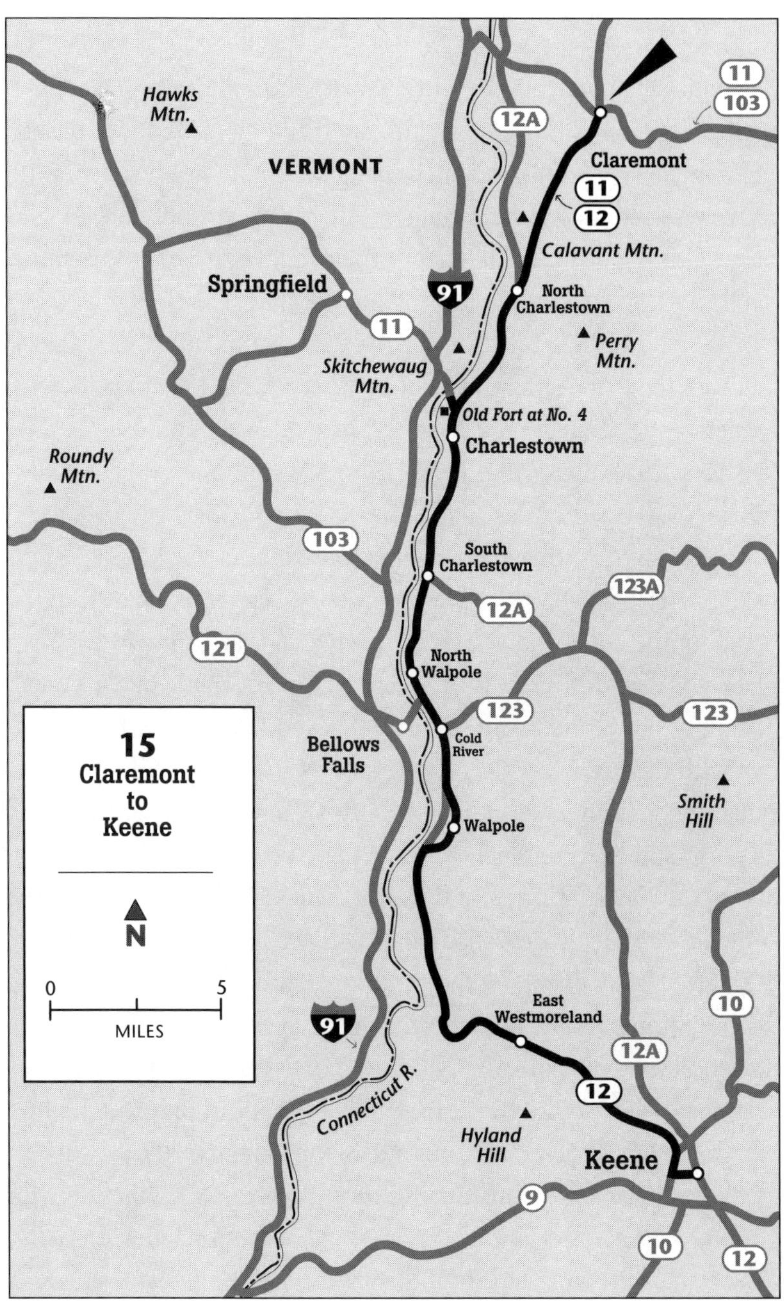
Hawks Mtn.
VERMONT
11
103
12A
Claremont
11
12
Calavant Mtn.
Springfield
91
North Charlestown
11
Perry Mtn.
Skitchewaug Mtn.
Old Fort at No. 4
Charlestown
Roundy Mtn.
103
South Charlestown
123A
12A
121
North Walpole
123
123
Bellows Falls
Cold River
15
Claremont to Keene
N
0
5
MILES
Smith Hill
Walpole
10
East Westmoreland
91
12A
12
Connecticut R.
Hyland Hill
Keene
9
10
12

Perry Mountain. If you look over your right shoulder, you'll see periodic good views of Hawks Mountain and other Vermont peaks. The long, steep profile of Skitchewaug Mountain lies just across the river in Vermont as you continue south. Open pastures and, in summer, fields of corn line the road to the east in a number of places.

NH 11 leaves to the right shortly as you near Charlestown. Take a brief side trip here on 11 to see the Old Fort at No. 4, near the banks of the Connecticut River. This stockaded colonial fort is a replica of the original built near here around 1744 and used as a defensive fortification during King George's War and the French and Indian Wars (see Charles Clark's *The Eastern Frontier*). "No. 4" was the name given to this grant by its proprietors in the Massachusetts Bay Colony. In 1744, there were only ten or eleven people sheltered here, but the community grew to nearly two hundred before the place was abandoned in the 1760s. The fort became a major point of supply, north and south, as troops moved in and out of the conflict with the French. The community was subject to almost constant Indian raids from its founding onward, with many residents either killed or abducted to Quebec. Some captives were redeemed for money and later returned to the settlement. The history of the fort comes alive in daily demonstrations and programs, which include costumed reenactments in the summer months. Beyond the fort site on Old Springfield Road you can cross to Springfield, Vermont, via the Cheshire Toll Bridge.

Coming back to US 12 south, you pass next through Charlestown village, by Breakneck Hill. Continue driving south to the Lower Meadows section of South Charlestown, then past the junction with NH 12A and across Hackett Brook. Many of these small western New Hampshire villages reflect the architecture of an earlier time.

Churches face the green at Walpole, New Hampshire.

Some still support the graceful old churches built a century ago. Inevitably, a few of these churches gained an awful reputation for the lengthy oratory heard within on Sundays. As accounts have it, one man fell asleep listening to his pastor's interminable exhortation. When he suddenly awoke, he whispered to the parishioner sitting next to him, "How long has he been preaching?" The fellow replied: "Oh, about thirty or forty years." "We'll, I guess I'll stay," the sleeper remarked. "He must be most through."

Your route now follows the Connecticut River more closely, with good water views as you drop southward to North Walpole, opposite Bellows Fall, Vermont. You will also spot Darby, Signal, and Jones Hills westward in Vermont above North Walpole. After passing the junction with NH 123 east at Cold River, continue south on NH 12 and NH 123 to Walpole. You will have further striking views of the green hills of Vermont to the west.

Here you leave NH 12 for a moment to enjoy the tranquil, attractive village of Walpole, just east of the highway. Watch for signs and *turn left* and *east* off 12, coming shortly into the village on Main Street. There are a number of fine buildings around the village center, well-preserved church spires, and a pretty green by the town offices. Park near the monument and walk around. Then *go east* on Main Street and take Wentworth Road southeast and uphill out of the town center. This byway takes you through real farm country, often cutting between house and barn. The hills are dotted with grazing cattle, and the pastures drift off into lovely, wooded uplands. You climb southward, crest the hill, pass several distinctive older homes, and descend past the silos of the Inn at Valley Farms (see also "An Author's Favorites," page 168), three miles from Walpole center. Watch for Blackjack Crossing just beyond the inn; *turn right* and follow this road west and out to NH 12 once again.

South of Walpole, your route pulls back and away from the river in Boggy Meadows, next running due south in more open country to Westmoreland Depot. There are excellent high, westward views along this stretch toward Vermont's Green Mountains. Here, in attractive, rolling countryside, NH 12 bears more southeast and follows Mill Brook through East Westmoreland and by the Indian Arrowhead Forest Preserve. Going by Grays Hill, the route—now identified as the Monadnock Highway—enters the Black Brook flowage and comes into Keene from the northwest, joining NH 9 and 10 west of Ashuelot River Park, near the banks of the winding Ashuelot River. A short distance southward, NH 9, 10, and 12 intersect West Street, which you may follow left into the center of Keene. The West Street exit is well marked as you approach from the north.

16

Route:

Around Mount Monadnock:
Hillsborough to Marlborough and Keene

Highway:

Routes 9, 31, 137, 123, US Route 202, Route 124

Distance:

47.5 miles (one way)

Hillsborough lies on the Contoocook River about twenty miles west of Concord, New Hampshire's state capital. It is the former residence of America's fourteenth president, Franklin Pierce, whose homestead is northwest of town on NH 31. The house, opulent for its time, was built in 1804 and is maintained today as a museum. Pierce was the only New Hampshireman to reach the presidency, and by all accounts it was not a job he relished. Not surprisingly, he wished himself home in the rolling country of central New Hampshire, and this drive may show you why.

We begin this long arc through southwestern New Hampshire on Hillsborough's Main Street, *following it west* and *southwest* as it becomes NH 31 and 9, sometimes referred to as Saw Mill Road. You shortly pass the access point to the Pierce Homestead on your right as you continue southwest, then go by Franklin Pierce Lake, beneath Campbell and Gibson Mountains. The road crosses Steels

Pond shortly, then comes into North Branch, where you *bear left* and *south* to continue on NH 31. Your route now runs south around Meetinghouse Hill through lovely open countryside to Antrim Center and, just beyond, Clinton Village. NH 31 pulls eastward here and joins with US 202 in Antrim.

You now *proceed south* on NH 31 and US 202 as the road runs along the banks of the Contoocook River briefly, then come into rural Bennington at a junction with NH 47. *Stay on US 202* south of Bennington and *take a right on NH 137*, which brings you through Hancock village by diminutive Norway Pond, at the foot of Norway Hill. Hancock's fine period architecture provides an excuse to pause and perhaps walk around this inviting village. Next, *take NH 123 south* and *rejoin US 202* to continue into North Village and Peterborough.

Peterborough is home to the world-famous MacDowell Colony and to Boston University's Sargent Camp. The village, situated in rolling countryside at the junction of the Contoocook and Nubanusit Rivers, is a place of fine old homes, cultural activity, and small manufacturing. The MacDowell Colony, founded in 1896 by Edward MacDowell and Marian Nevins MacDowell, plays host to writers, musicians, and artists from all over the United States and around the world who come to work in a creative and supportive atmosphere. Peterborough's Town House draws its architectural inspiration from Boston's Faneuil Hall, and the town's old Unitarian Church, built in 1824, was designed by famed Boston architect Charles Bulfinch. In the 1840s Brigham Young assumed control of the fledgling Mormon Church here in Peterborough upon the death of its founder, Joseph Smith. One hundred thirty-six citizens of this region joined Young as he marched toward the promised land

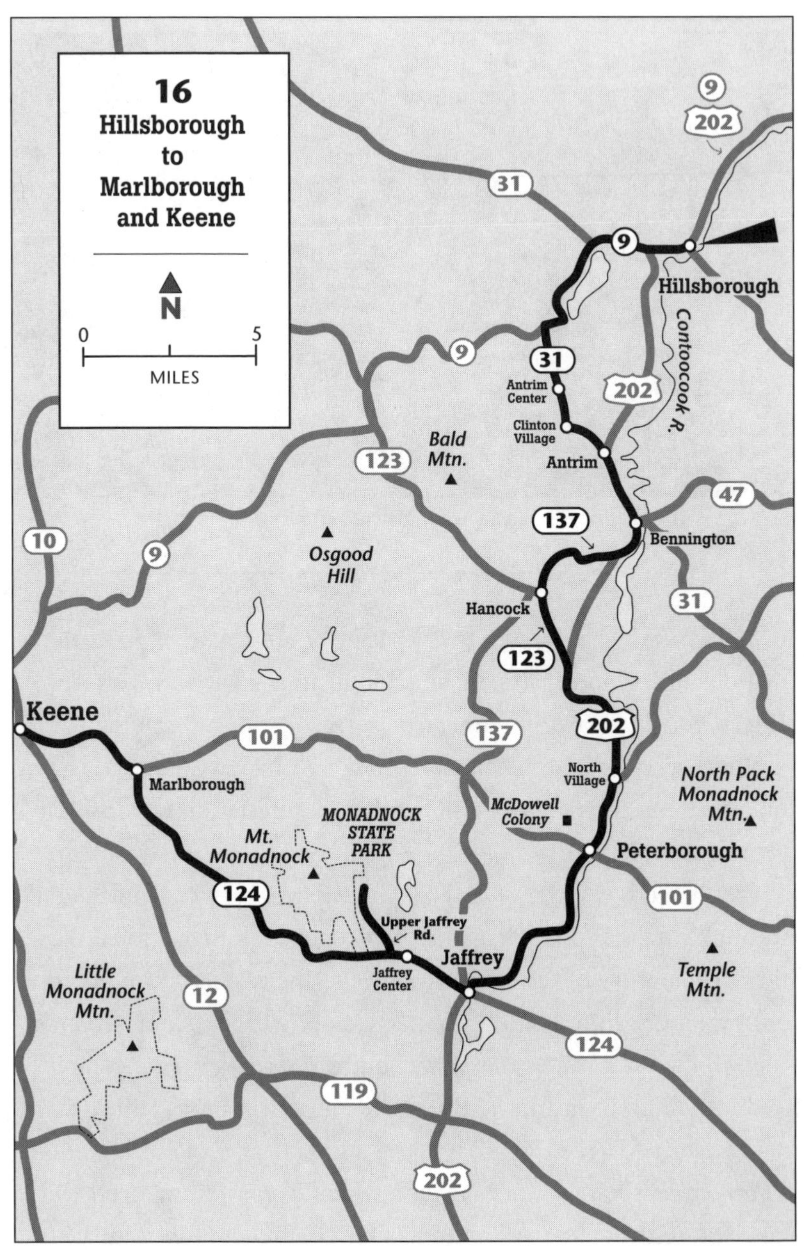
16
Hillsborough
to
Marlborough
and Keene
N
0
5
MILES
9
202
31
9
Hillsborough
Contoocook R.
9
31
Antrim Center
202
Clinton Village
Antrim
123
Bald Mtn.
47
137
Bennington
10
9
Osgood Hill
Hancock
31
123
Keene
202
101
137
Marlborough
North Village
North Pack Monadnock Mtn.
McDowell Colony
MONADNOCK STATE PARK
Mt. Monadnock
Peterborough
124
101
Upper Jaffrey Rd.
Jaffrey
Jaffrey Center
Little Monadnock Mtn.
12
Temple Mtn.
124
119
202

The historic Wyman Tavern in downtown Keene

in Utah on what proved to be a journey of great hardship. Textile manufacturing and scattered, small industries have been part of Peterborough's growth. There are accommodations, restaurants, and motorist services here. The Peterborough Historical Society Museum, on Grove Street, is a must-visit for those interested in regional history, well preserved.

From Peterborough, *follow US 202 southwest* for a few miles through rural countryside along the Contoocook River. You'll see the high country of the Wapack Range to the east as you proceed to Jaffrey, on Cheshire Pond. An attractive old village, Jaffrey is a crossroads for several routes that serve southwestern New Hampshire and is the hub to nearby Monadnock State Park. From Jaffrey, *drive northwest on NH 124*.

You come soon to Jaffrey Center, where Upper Jaffrey Road will take you to the state park and trails for climbing Mount Monadnock. This great, 3,165-foot mountain sees numerous climbers in most seasons and has had its praises sung in many a story. Its flavor was best captured in verse, I think, in poet Galway Kinnell's 1964 collection *Flower Herding on Mount Monadnock*. Besides a network of hiking trails, the park has seasonal primitive camping and Nordic skiing. These attractive evergreen woodlands merit a visit even if you do not hike to higher ground. Maps of trail routes and other information are available at the park entrance. Monadnock is surrounded by several bodies of water, including Thorndike Pond, Perkins Pond, Stone Pond, and Dublin Lake.

Once back on NH 124, go farther west through Cummings Meadow, skirting Monadnock and pulling gradually more northwest toward Marlborough, in hill country. The route travels through a marsh in wooded backcountry, passes the Rocky Ridge Trail to the big mountain, then turns due north by West Hill to the center of Marlborough, on Minnewawa and Robbins Brooks.

From Marlborough, it is only a short drive west on NH 101 to Keene. The final miles take you around Beech Hill Preserve to a junction with NH 12 and 12A (Main Street). *Turn right and north* on Main Street where you can end this journey a few blocks north of Keene State College at the Wyman Tavern, the meeting site of Revolutionary minutemen who marched from here to Concord, Massachusetts, in the spring of 1775.

From Keene, there are other connecting excursions in this book (see Routes #14, #15, and #18 on pages 111, 117 and 135).

17

Route:

An Uplands Journey: Keene to Charlestown

Highway:

Routes 12A, 123A

Distance:

32 miles (one way)

This route winds through the hill ranges of southwestern New Hampshire from Keene to Charlestown on a series of high, isolated country roads with good outlooks and sections of attractive streamside travel. The drive will take you through tiny rural settlements that maintain the flavor of an unspoiled New Hampshire and an untrammeled place. These routes are, too, nearly devoid of cars. You'll have the road pretty much to yourself.

From the high end of Keene's interesting Main Street, follow Court Street, an area of attractive older houses, west out of town, passing Ashuelot River Park on your left. The road gradually enters rural countryside with occasional ridgeline views and passes the site of the old Cheshire Turnpike stone arch bridge. At the junction about two and a half miles from downtown Keene, *go right* and *north* on NH 12A. Here you begin to enjoy occasional views to higher, wooded ridgelines to the right, the earliest of a series of hills and ridges you will follow north on this drive. Houses are few, and tall hardwoods arch over the road as you enter Surry. Opposite Bear Den Hill you pass Surry Dam Road to the right, leading to Surry Mountain Lake Recreational Area; you are now five and a half miles from Keene's Main Street. Surry Mountain forms the elongated ridge to the immediate northeast.

As you cross Merriam and Fuller Brooks, then skirt a bend in the Ashuelot River, you'll see views opening up to the hills farther northeast, and, in summer, an intervale grown up in corn. Pastures dot the intervale beyond the screen of trees as you go through Shaws Corner. You cross the Alstead town line (ten miles now from Keene) amid more pasture backed by hills. Here the route slabs along a shelf on the side of Marvin Hill to your left, climbing steadily up and over a rise. You'll next descend northward into Alstead Center by Beaver Wood Pond and take in fine views off to the right over open pasture near Prentice Hill. After a long, northward descent, NH 12A joins NH 123 shortly. In less than a mile, after following Warren Brook northwest and west nearly into Alstead village, you leave both roads and *bear right on NH 123A*.

Go northeast now on NH 123A, past a waterfall spanned by a footbridge at Vilas Pool, and come to the old Langdon Bridge, a covered structure awaiting repairs and restoration. The road winds frequently as it pulls eastward and stays along the Cold River, which it crosses in a few minutes. The river makes an attractive foil to the surrounding greenery. It drops gradually into a gorge to your right where it has eroded a channel. Pass Tamarack Farm, where maple syrup is made and sold. Winding back and forth again, the road and river head more northeastward between Osgood Ledge

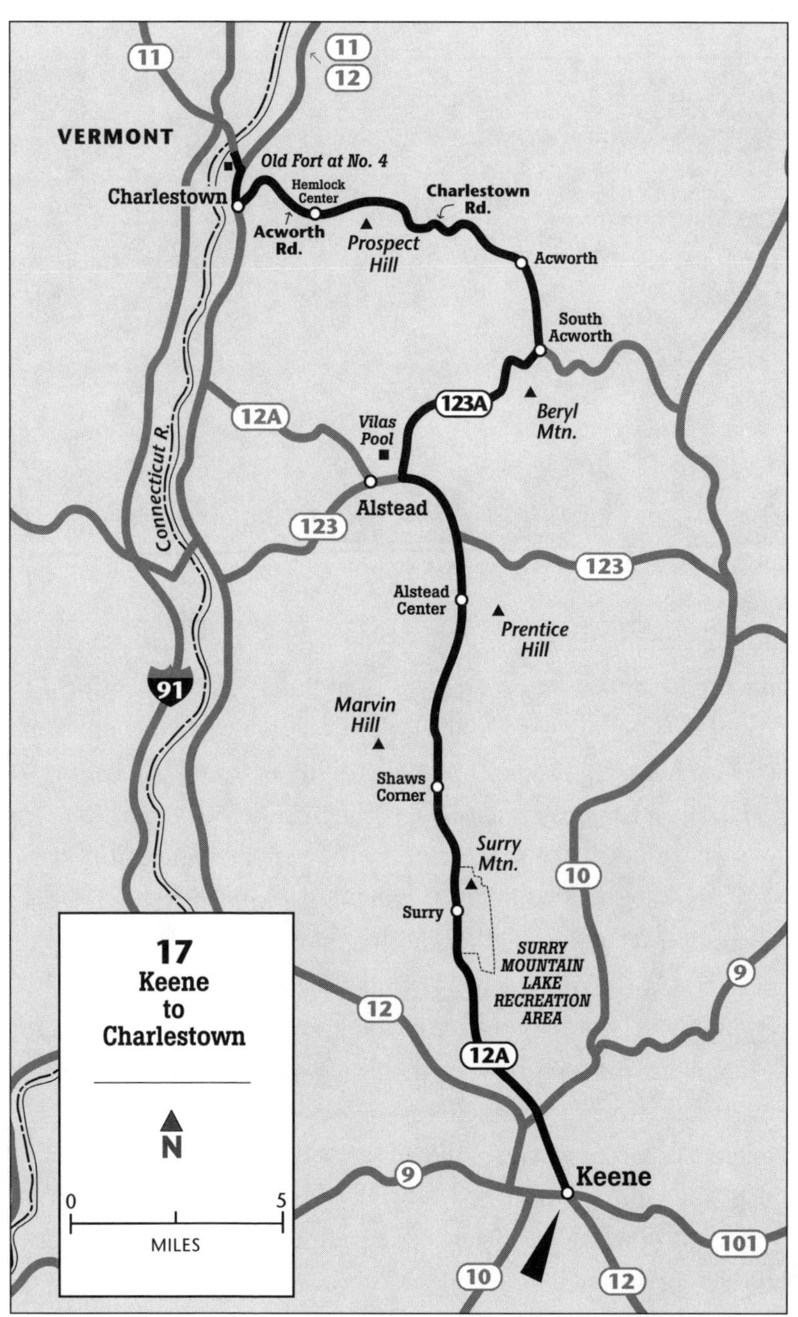
11
11
12
VERMONT
Old Fort at No. 4
Charlestown
Hemlock Center
Acworth Rd.
Prospect Hill
Charlestown Rd.
Acworth
South Acworth
123A
Beryl Mtn.
12A
Vilas Pool
Alstead
123
123
Connecticut R.
Alstead Center
Prentice Hill
91
Marvin Hill
Shaws Corner
Surry Mtn.
10
Surry
SURRY MOUNTAIN LAKE RECREATION AREA
9
12
12A
9
Keene
101
10
12
17
Keene
to
Charlestown
N
0
5
MILES

Town and church buildings at Acworth

and Beryl Mountain, then cross Milliken Brook. After traversing a beautiful, sweeping bend in the Cold River, you come to a junction at South Acworth, twenty-two and a half miles from your starting point. There is a small bridge just to the right here. From it, you can see west into the deep gorge worn by the current over centuries.

At the junction of Hill Street, *turn sharply left and north* toward Acworth, leaving the Cold River. The route now climbs quickly north and northwest in woods and pasturelands, momentarily passing the Acworth Volunteer Fire and Rescue Station. Traveling farther along the high ridge, you arrive in just a couple of miles at Acworth. Above a broad green, the Acworth Town Hall, the United Church of Acworth, the little Acworth Center School, and the Silsby Library are clustered together, pleasant anachronisms in the midst of the heavily wooded countryside that stretches for miles in all directions.

From this quiet junction in Acworth, *go left* and *northwest* on the Charlestown Road, crossing Milliken Brook again and following a series of fine stone walls. Collector hoses and other signs of maple sugar operations lie in the woods alongside the road. This is a narrow, up-and-down road, and cars are as scarce as hen's teeth. It is the kind of road that one dreams of when stuck in a traffic jam in any major city. In New Hampshire, there are, indeed, plenty of such roads.

Continue northwest, then west as the route negotiates a series of bends and begins to descend. Occasional brief, distant views of mountains in Vermont are seen ahead. Some high pasture comes and goes, and more ridgeline outlooks to the west occur now. Human settlement is sparse, with only an occasional house or farmstead at the roadside. Descending some more, the route soon runs through a farmyard—the house on one side of the road, the barn on the other—as it skirts Prospect Hill. More curves present themselves as you wind through pastures and orchards in the direction of Charlestown. Groves of hemlock populate a place called, not surprisingly, Hemlock Center.

As the road widens, you drop west once more, with good views ahead to some of the high summits in Vermont. The route is named Acworth Road as you enter a settlement, negotiate more turns, then arrive in open fields grown up in corn in summer. *Go left* shortly on the Old Claremont Road, which you ride southwest just a short distance to the village of Charlestown, on the Connecticut River, and the junction with NH 12.

The Old Fort at No. 4 is located here. The restoration of this northernmost fortified settlement under British control in the mid-1700s is open to visitors seasonally. It is easily reached a half mile

The Old Fort at No. 4, Charlestown

north of the village center on NH 11 (Old Springfield Road). You also may cross to Springfield, Vermont, via the Cheshire Toll Bridge on this side road. From Charlestown it is possible to drive south to Keene on NH 12 or north to Claremont on NH 11 and 12 (see Route #15, page 117).

18

Route:
A Cheshire County Loop

Highway:
Routes 12, 119, 32, 9

Distance:
40 miles (one way)

A short ramble through some of the back roads of New Hampshire's southwestern corner, close to the Massachusetts and Vermont state lines, will pay fine dividends. Village architecture, covered bridges, interesting natural formations, and appealing hill country characterize this quiet area. The route leaves Keene, southwestern New Hampshire's largest community, and heads south to Fitzwilliam, runs west to Richmond, then climbs north again via Swanzey. Along the way it passes through several attractive villages, skirts dozens of rolling hills, and even meanders through river and marsh country.

Begin this tour in Keene on NH 12, which departs the south side of the city as Main Street. NH 12 drops southeast from the built-up area, skirts Wilson Pond, and passes the Cheshire Fairgrounds, on the right. Running between Forbush and Marcy Hills, your route then crosses Forbush Brook. Hills and ridges clothed in mixed hardwoods lie to the southwest along here. Your route continues to the southeast, passing Farrar Pond and coming to the village of Troy at an intersection with Jaffrey Road. With outlooks left and southwest to Little Monadnock Mountain, NH 12 rounds a marsh that feeds Bowker Pond, then comes to Fitzwilliam village.

This appealing community, well set up in period architecture, is the intersection of several rural routes that transect the southwestern New Hampshire countryside. It is home to the Amos Blake House, an impressive structure built in 1837 and now preserved as a museum by the Fitzwilliam Historical Society. Set opposite the Fitzwilliam Inn, the Blake House is open for viewing seasonally. Fitzwilliam's center surrounds a traditional village green with churches and meetinghouses, a pleasing sight regardless of season and reminiscent of another time. A walk around the green makes a nice break in this journey.

From the village green, *follow NH 119 west* to Fitzwilliam Depot, where the road skirts, then crosses a large marsh. Rhododendron Road is on your right as you depart Fitzwilliam Depot, and you may wish to leave the main highway and follow this side route to Rhododendron State Park, at Little Monadnock Mountain. The park can also be accessed via Daley Road, off 119 west of Fitzwilliam Depot. There are more than sixteen acres of wild rhododendrons growing here, in full blossom with vibrant color by mid-July. The park has a series of trails, viewing areas, and a natural area.

Continue west on NH 119, crossing Kemp Brook and going through Beechwood Corners. You then cross Boyce and Tully Brooks, which drain a lengthy bog and series of ponds to the north. NH 119 is an up-and-down road as it drifts westward around Grassy Hill to a crossroads with NH 32 at Richmond. This is lightly

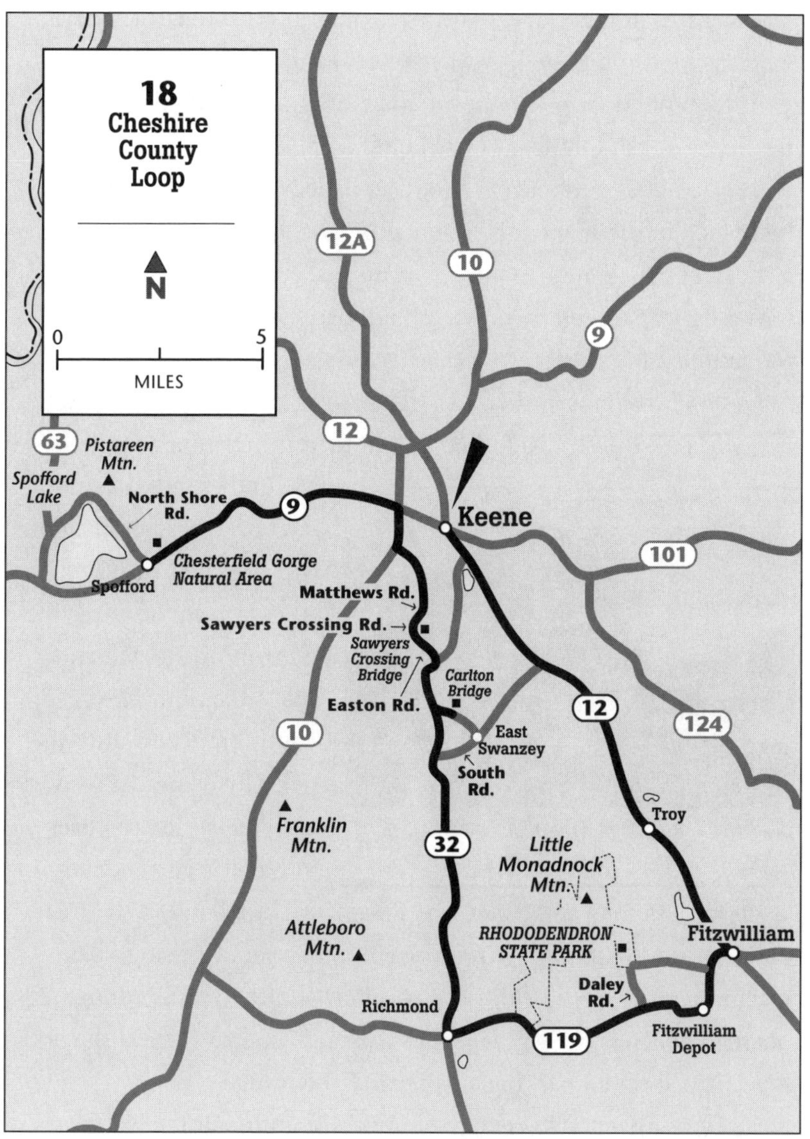
18
Cheshire
County
Loop
N
0
5
MILES
12A
10
9
12
63
Pistareen
Mtn.
Spofford
Lake
North Shore
Rd.
9
Keene
Chesterfield Gorge
Natural Area
Spofford
101
Matthews Rd.
Sawyers Crossing Rd.
Sawyers
Crossing
Bridge
Carlton
Bridge
Easton Rd.
12
124
10
East
Swanzey
South
Rd.
Troy
Franklin
Mtn.
32
Little
Monadnock
Mtn.
Attleboro
Mtn.
RHODODENDRON
STATE PARK
Fitzwilliam
Daley
Rd.
Richmond
119
Fitzwilliam
Depot

settled country of marsh, mixed fields, and dense woodlands draped over a series of low ridges. The acres of uninterrupted, thick hardwood groves lining the highway are brilliant in autumn.

At Richmond, *bear right* at the junction and *head north on NH 32*, passing a marsh that feeds Cass Pond. NH 32 is a quiet rural road with occasional outlooks westward to Attleboro Mountain and other highlands in the Franconia Mountains. The road meanders through a series of marshlands that are part of Rice and Martin Brooks. Off to the right, particularly in winter, are periodic glimpses of Little Monadnock Mountain.

As NH 32 climbs farther into the western precincts of East Swanzey, you pass South Road, then continue north less than a mile to a sign that indicates a covered bridge. A short side trip *right* and *eastward* takes you to the attractive Carlton Bridge, which spans the diminutive South Branch of the Ashuelot River amidst woods and fields. Coming back to NH 32, *go right* and *north* for less than two miles, then *take a left* at a bend in the road onto Easton Road, then *go right* again on Sawyers Crossing Road, reaching the covered bridge of that name shortly. This is a long, red-boarded covered bridge that spans the main course of the Ashuelot River. You'll find a parking area next to the bridge.

The Carlton Bridge in Swanzey

Head west over Sawyers Crossing Bridge and look for Matthews Road, where you *go right* and *north*, continuing to a junction with

Several covered bridges lie south of Keene, this one at Sawyer's Crossing.

NH 10. *Go right on 10* and travel it briefly to its junction with NH 9 and 12, the Franklin Pierce Highway. *Turn left* and *west* and travel NH 9 roughly five miles to the Spofford section of Chesterfield, next to Pistareen Mountain and Spofford Lake. Just before you come into Spofford, watch for signs to the Chesterfield Gorge Natural Area. Pause for a while at this small, thirteen-acre park. You'll find a walking trail through interesting formations of metamorphic rock shaped by years of water action and weathering. A seasonal nature center is located here, too. Nearby NH 9A and Shore Road provide an attractive shore drive around Spofford Lake, in the shadow of Pistareen Mountain. A short drive east on NH 9 brings you back to Keene.

19

Route:

A Lakes Region Route: Franklin to Holderness

Highway:

Route 3A, Routes 104, local roads, US Route 3

Distance:

35.5 miles (one way)

A back roads drive around the lakes of this lovely region is sometimes in order. This route will take you from the old, established town of Franklin to Bristol, east to Meredith, then north to Ashland and Holderness, passing a number of lakes, large and small, along the way. Despite their meander through New Hampshire's popular Lakes Region, these roads usually are not crowded and make attractive routes for touring. This drive is good at any time of the year, but is especially inviting in high summer or in autumn, with the explosion of colorful foliage.

Begin this journey at the junction of NH 11 and 3A in West Franklin. *Go north* here on 3A, leaving the business section, then going through a rock cut and passing the Franklin Falls Dam, point of formation for New England's historic Merrimack River. There are excellent views northeastward here over the dam and on toward Calef Hill. Less than six miles along, you pass through the center of

Hill, with the long, marshy backwater of the Franklin Falls Reservoir to the right through the trees. This body of water is formed by the inflow of the Pemigewasset River and Bennett, Knox, Needle Shop, Prescott, and Blake Brooks.

The road now rolls through corridors of closely grown hardwoods with occasional views of mountains ahead. Open pastures dot the landscape periodically. North of Hill, the road runs west briefly, then climbs straight north near Periwig Mountain and around Foster Swamp. You pass the side road to Profile Falls on the right as you cross the town line into Bristol, at just under ten miles from Franklin, then come into town on South Main Street and cross the Newfound River.

Established in 1819, Bristol lies just a couple of miles below the south end of Newfound Lake and is the major shopping area for communities around the lake. The town is the site of Sugar Hill State Forest and Kelly Park. A short side trip up NH 3A from the town center will bring you to the south shore of the lake and a public beach.

From Bristol's downtown area, *go right* and *east* on NH 104 (Summer Street, becoming River Road). You leave Bristol's settled area rapidly and move east, with hill views before you in rolling countryside. As the road dips between a cluster of hills, you pass the regional hospital and take in views on the right of the impounded waters of the Pemigewasset River, behind Ayers Island Dam, fifteen miles from Franklin. Outlooks to Burleigh, Hersey, and Sanbornton Mountains are to the southeast. Sixteen and a half miles from your starting point, watch for a side road that goes by the New Hampton School. The small, attractive campus of this old private academy dominates the town of New Hampton. After driving through the

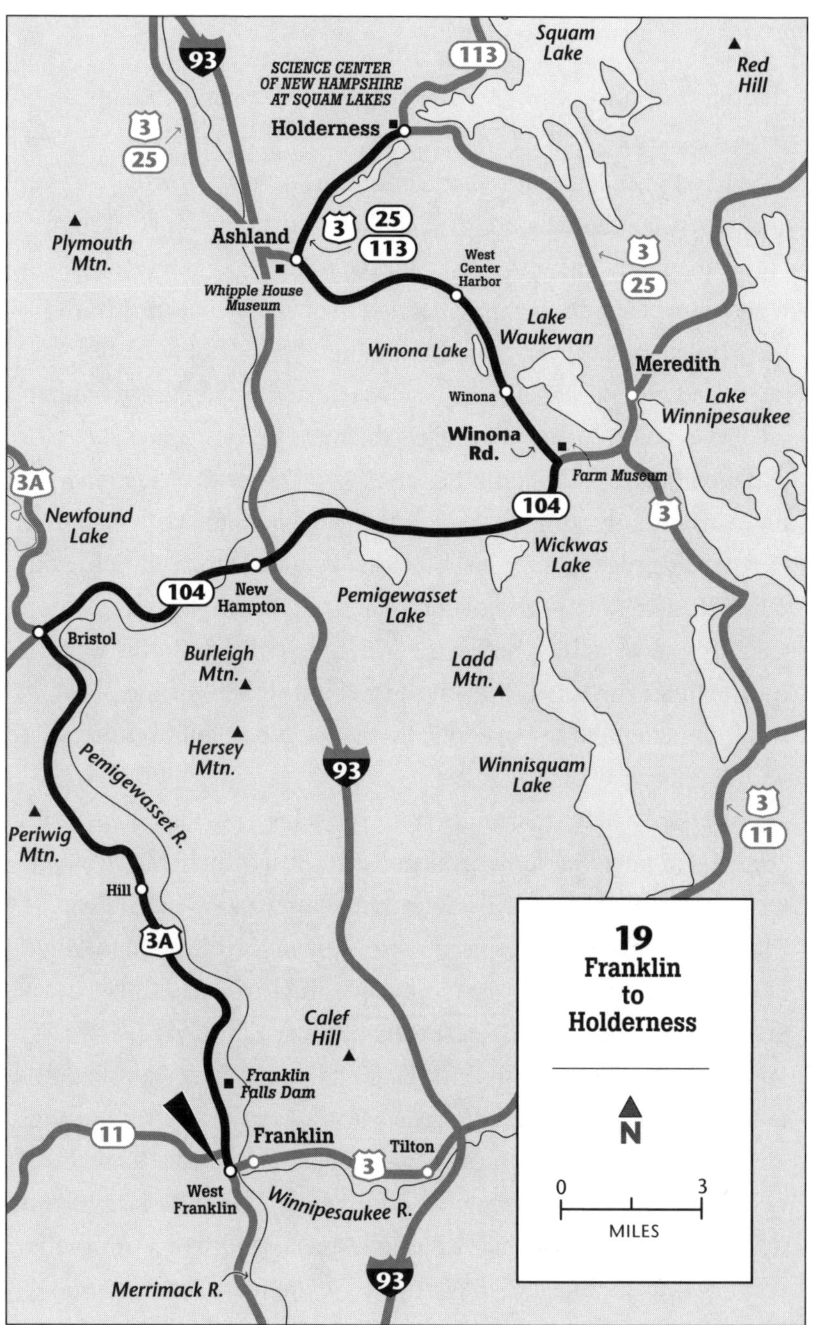

93
SCIENCE CENTER
OF NEW HAMPSHIRE
AT SQUAM LAKES
113
Squam
Lake
Red
Hill
Holderness
3
25
Plymouth
Mtn.
Ashland
3
25
113
Whipple House
Museum
West
Center
Harbor
3
25
Lake
Waukewan
Winona Lake
Meredith
Winona
Lake
Winnipesaukee
Winona
Rd.
Farm Museum
3A
104
3
Newfound
Lake
Wickwas
Lake
104
New
Hampton
Pemigewasset
Lake
Bristol
Burleigh
Mtn.
Ladd
Mtn.
Hersey
Mtn.
Pemigewasset R.
93
Winnisquam
Lake
Periwig
Mtn.
3
11
Hill
3A
19
Franklin
to
Holderness
Calef
Hill
Franklin
Falls Dam
N
11
Franklin
Tilton
3
0
3
MILES
West
Franklin
Winnipesaukee R.
Merrimack R.
93

campus, reconnect with NH 104 at the end of Main Street by the underpass for I-93.

NH 104 goes under I-93 and continues eastward in a built-up area. Driving gradually out of this unattractive developed section, you come to Pemigewasset Lake on the right; there is a turnout where you can stop to enjoy the water views. The lake feeds into the Pemigewasset River, which flows from considerably farther north and around Lincoln; its headwaters are in the great mountain wilderness of the same name. Pass the Meredith town line at twenty and a half miles from Franklin. Shortly you come to a side road on the right indicating Wickwas Lake. Turn in here briefly and follow the side road east for a short distance, where there are pleasant outlooks over this lovely, small lake and, beyond it, Winnisquam Lake. In the years long before the widening of US 104, this was a quiet, almost unvisited spot, and one could sit here by the only store, as I often did in boyhood summers, peering out over the lakes with hardly a car passing.

Just under twenty-four miles from Franklin, you climb a rise and come to an intersection, where you turn left by White Mountain Orthopedics on what has been for years known as Winona Road. The road is unsigned, but head north here in the direction of Waukewan, ascending a hill past a cemetery and the Meredith Historical Society Farm Museum (open seasonally; check for hours). The road winds and descends northward, passing the Old Print Barn before reaching a junction with Waukewan Road. Continue north on Winona Road, crest a hill, and descend steeply to an unusual, blind railroad overpass. (Sounding the horn before cautiously heading under was something we always did here years ago.) In a few minutes you begin to skirt beautiful Winona Lake, on the left, with views

The green at Hebron, New Hampshire

down a marsh to the southeast on your right, where the connecting flow leads to Lake Waukewan. The road enters West Center Harbor, then follows the lake northward past cottages. On many a summer morning in my youth, I would row the length of this lake to the northeast corner to buy milk and eggs from a farmer who kept cows and chickens. When I reached home, the eggs and fresh milk would go into an old icebox fed with great blocks of ice from an icehouse at the Mayo Farm on the Waukewan Road.

The route winds around the north end of Winona Lake in a series of narrow, sharp curves, then heads gradually toward Ashland, following an abandoned railroad line. Crack express trains for Canada once flew through here. After crossing the New Hampton town line and going by the Haus Trillium Pottery, you quickly come to Ashland near Ames Brook Campground and drive into the village center itself. Ashland was once the home of George Hoyt Whipple, a medical doctor and researcher who garnered the 1934 Nobel Prize for medicine for his work on treating pernicious anemia. His twelve-room brick house, built in 1837, has been preserved as a museum of local history. It is worth a visit while you are here.

From the junction with US 3 and NH 25 in the center of Ashland, *turn right* and northeast on US 3 along the outlet stream of Little Squam Lake. There are several points with outlooks over Little Squam as you travel eastward here, and the lake widens as you progress. Far across the lake is Shepard Hill. There are a number of resorts and other accommodations along this stretch of road. In minutes, you rise at a bend and come into the small but busy crossroads of Holderness. Here, at the end of this drive, you will find not only water views over both Little and Big Squam Lakes (the latter east of town) but also the Science Center of New Hampshire at Squam Lakes, a nature center and educational facility teaching ecological awareness through exploration of local natural sites. The center also supports a wildlife refuge.

From Holderness, US 3 and NH 25 will take you eastward to the town of Meredith. Or NH 113 will take you northeastward around Squam Lake in the shadow of the mountains of the attractive Squam Range to Center Sandwich.

20

Route:
Franklin–Mount Kearsarge Loop

Highway:
US Route 3, Routes 127, local roads,103, 114, 11

Distance:
49.5 miles

A drive through the rolling lakes and hill country of west-central New Hampshire is a means to collecting small towns. They are everywhere: Salisbury, Warner, North Sutton, Wilmot Flat, Potter Place, Andover. This route visits all of them, including the pretty college town of New London and the interesting river settlement of Franklin. Many of these little villages were left behind with the construction of nearby I-89. Today, they are minor oases of traditional New Hampshire life and architecture, often maintaining an established community focus amidst the gradual encroachment of all that is modern. This route will also carry you in a full circle around the great rise of Mount Kearsarge, almost 3,000 feet high and one of the two most prominent uplands in this part of the state.

Begin your journey this time in Franklin, most easily reached via I-93 from Exits 19 or 20 at Tilton. Alternatively, you can approach Franklin from the north or south on US 3, which runs right through the town. Franklin, birthplace of Daniel Webster, saw its first white inhabitants in 1761 and was incorporated as a town in 1828; it did not become a city until more than a half century later, in 1895. The community was established at the confluence of the Pemigewasset and Winnipesaukee Rivers by Ebeneezer Eastman and was originally part of Salisbury. For many years Franklin was a center of small manufacturing and has become a retail center for nearby Lakes Region resort communities.

Franklin was a natural mill site in its earliest days, the collecting point of the Pemigewasset, Winnipesaukee, and Newfound Rivers and of Bennett, Cate, Knox, and Weeks Brooks, plus other small streams to the north, whose combined flow—now controlled by the Franklin Falls Dam—gives birth to the robust Merrimack River. Like so many settlements in early New England, Franklin owed its origins to water and the power it offered.

To get under way, *drive south* from Franklin on US 3, *turning right* and *southwest* in a mile on NH 127 toward Salisbury. Rolling through rural countryside now, watch for North Road on the right less than two miles farther west on NH 127. A short run *right* and *north* up this side road brings you to the humble birthplace of American statesman and sometime New Hampshireman Daniel Webster. Born in 1782, Webster was, in fact, elected to national office only once by his New Hampshire peers, but he continued to exert his significant influence on early national affairs from other venues. This simple, two-room house with period accoutrements is on a 172-acre state reservation.

Back on NH 127, you *proceed southwest* in rural woodlands and fields between Searles Hill and Smith Hill, passing through a junction with US 4 in Salisbury and continuing to Warner Road. Take

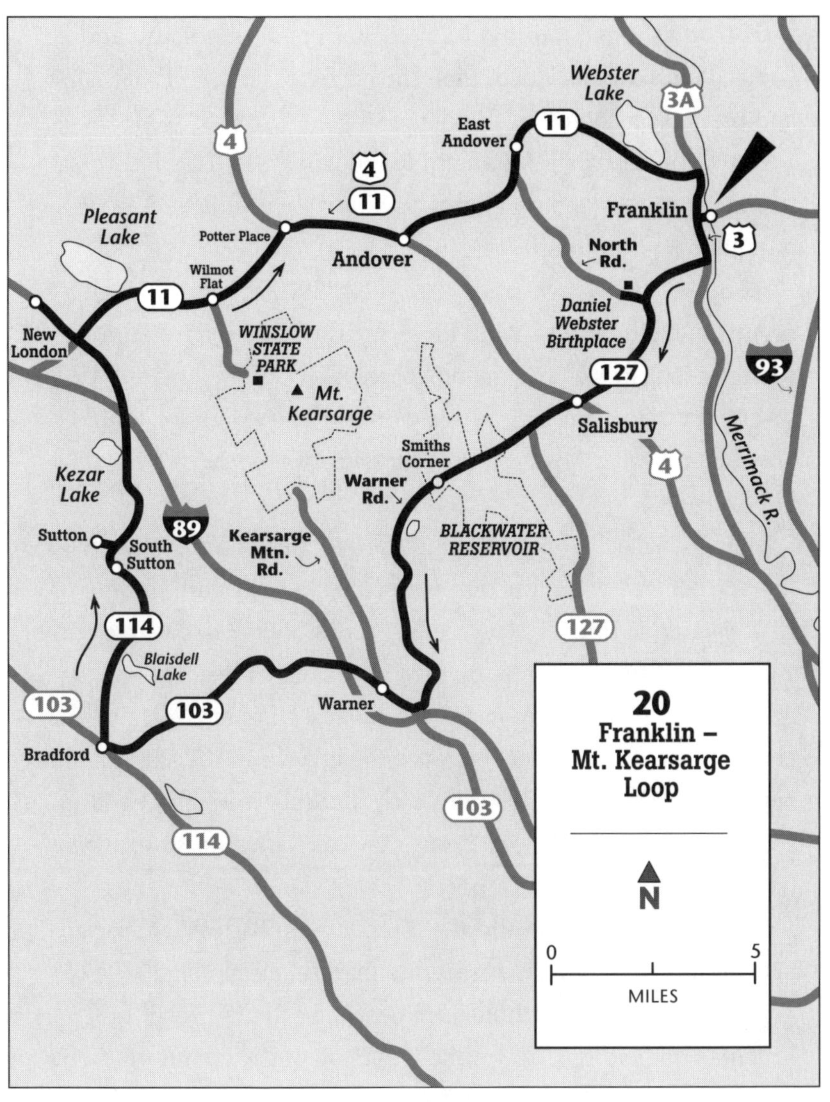
Webster Lake
3A
East Andover
11
4
4
11
Franklin
3
Pleasant Lake
Potter Place
Andover
North Rd.
Wilmot Flat
11
Daniel Webster Birthplace
New London
WINSLOW STATE PARK
Mt. Kearsarge
127
93
Salisbury
Smiths Corner
4
Merrimack R.
Kezar Lake
Warner Rd.
89
BLACKWATER RESERVOIR
Sutton
South Sutton
Kearsarge Mtn. Rd.
127
114
Blaisdell Lake
103
103
Warner
Bradford
103
114
20
Franklin – Mt. Kearsarge Loop
N
0
5
MILES

Warner Road *to the right* and *west* across the Blackwater Reservoir flowage to the hamlet of Smiths Corner. Stay with this winding rural road as it goes around little Tucker Pond, dips south and becomes Pumpkin Hill Road, then travels over the rise of that name and brings you soon into Warner.

Watch for Kearsarge Mountain Road in Warner. This local side trip takes you to an auto road that climbs the south side of the mountain and on to Rollins State Park.

From Warner, *go right* and *west* on NH 103, driving through pretty, rolling terrain to Waterloo, a country crossroads that long ago took its name to commemorate the Duke of Wellington's victory several thousand miles away. A side trip of a few hundred yards down Newmarket Road, on the left, takes you to the site of Waterloo Bridge.

Back on NH 103, you now run through Melvin Mills, then follow the Warner River to a junction with NH 114 just south of Bradford. *Go right* and *north* on 114, skirting a series of ponds, passing Wright and Dodge Hills, and crossing several streams to reach South Sutton. Beautiful Mount Kearsarge, the highest peak in the region, lies to the northeast, and there are occasional views of the summit along here. NH 114 next wraps itself nearly around Meetinghouse Hill, goes by attractive Gile Pond and Kezar Lake, then heads into New London via Main Street.

Colby-Sawyer College and the New London Barn Playhouse are here, as are accommodations, eating places, and motorist services. The town hall and courthouse are near the campus. You'll find Knights Hill Nature Park on the west side of the community on Lakeside Road. A break in your journey for a walk around the village might be refreshing. New London possesses the kind of

The Cold River meanders eastward at South Acworth.

modest scale and charm that one automatically thinks of in a small New England college town.

From New London, take NH 11 northeast from Crockett Corner, heading toward Wilmot Flat, driving south of Pleasant Lake (fishing and boating access), and passing hidden Chase and Tannery Ponds on your left. On your right now, Old Winslow Road and Kearsarge Valley Road provide access south to Winslow State Park and a network of hiking trails that reach the summit of Mount Kearsarge. You come to the Cilleyville Bridge beyond Wilmot Flat and, a few miles farther, connect with US 4 at Potter Place. US 4 and NH 11 run east together for a while and soon lead to Keniston Bridge in Andover by the Blackwater River. Potter Place, Wilmot Flat, and Andover are miniature villages of the type common in an older, less developed New Hampshire and now fast disappearing. Poet Donald Hall talks of such places in *Life Work*. Ragged Mountain Ski Area is to the north of Andover. Both Ragged Mountain and the formation known as the Bulkhead lie to your left.

NH 11 pulls leftward and away from US 4 just beyond Andover. Watch for a turn by a cut in some granitic ledges. *Stay with NH 11* and go east near the Horseshoe Ponds in more pleasing rural countryside bordered by tall groves of pine. You soon go by hidden Elbow Pond and, with the road bearing sharply to the northeast, round hidden Highland Lake in East Andover (fishing and boating access). The Congregational meetinghouse sits on a rise to the right of the road. Tucker Mountain and Bald Hill loom above the lake to the northwest.

Hillside farms dot the countryside as you wend eastward. The route next traverses Sucker Brook, crosses the Franklin town line, and makes a run down the west side of Webster Lake (fishing and boating access), with fine, expansive water views. A low range of hills caps the view across the water. In minutes you pass Legace Beach, then join with NH 3A in West Franklin. Take 11 and 3A south to US 3 (Central Street) at the Daniel Webster Bridge to cross the Merrimack to Franklin and the end of this journey.

21

Route:

Goffstown to Keene

Highway:

Routes 13, 136, US 202, Route 101, local roads

Distance:

45 miles (one way)

This journey begins near New Hampshire's historically important industrial city of Manchester, wends its way west to scenic Peterborough, then through a series of picturesque little hamlets in southwestern New Hampshire to the college town of Keene, hub of Cheshire County. Before you set out, you'll find it rewarding to spend some time in Manchester, which offers glimpses of early industrial history, access to the fine arts, and other interesting sites.

New Hampshire's largest city and home of the great Amoskeag mills, Manchester was once the largest cotton manufactory in the world. It is still the state's commercial center. The region was first explored by Europeans in 1636 under the aegis of Massachusetts Bay Colony governor Winthrop. The city obtained its charter as Derryfield from Governor Benning Wentworth in 1751. Manchester lies next to Amoskeag Falls, once an Indian gathering place where Englishman John Eliot came to preach to the tribes in 1650. With a large Franco-American population, and a significant Greek, Polish, and Irish cultural heritage, the Queen City grew up on textile and shoe manufacturing. The great mills were fed with waterpower in a canal system completed in 1807. Manchester is also home to the Currier Gallery of Art, a fine collection of classical and international art plus works from New Hampshire and New England artists housed in a building designed by Tilden and Githens in 1927. The Frank Lloyd Wright designed Zimmerman Building is here, too. To get a sense of the city's unique history, visit the Manchester Historical Association's museum on Amherst Street. Campuses of the University of New Hampshire system, Notre Dame College, and the New Hampshire Vocational-Technical Institute are also located here.

To reach Goffstown, *proceed west* from Manchester on NH 114A, which crosses the Queen City Bridge and (as Mast Road) winds its way westward out of the built-up area along the banks of the Piscataquog River in the Pinardville section of the city. You reach Goffstown shortly beyond the junction of NH 114 and 114A. In the center of Goffstown, at the monument, NH 114 joins NH 13, which you *follow south* through the square, then right and west toward Crotched Mountain. Driving west and southwest, you stay on the south side of the Piscataquog River as you approach New Boston. Coming quickly into rural countryside, the route skirts Browns Hill and a large marsh while turning more southwest. The road follows the river closely here, bend for bend. Occasional turnouts line the riverbank along this attractive stretch.

In the little crossroads of New Boston, with its neat rows of older houses, you come to the junction of NH 136 and 77. Before leaving NH 13 and *going west* on NH 136, you may wish to pause here for a short side trip to Joe English Hill, farther along NH 13. Heading

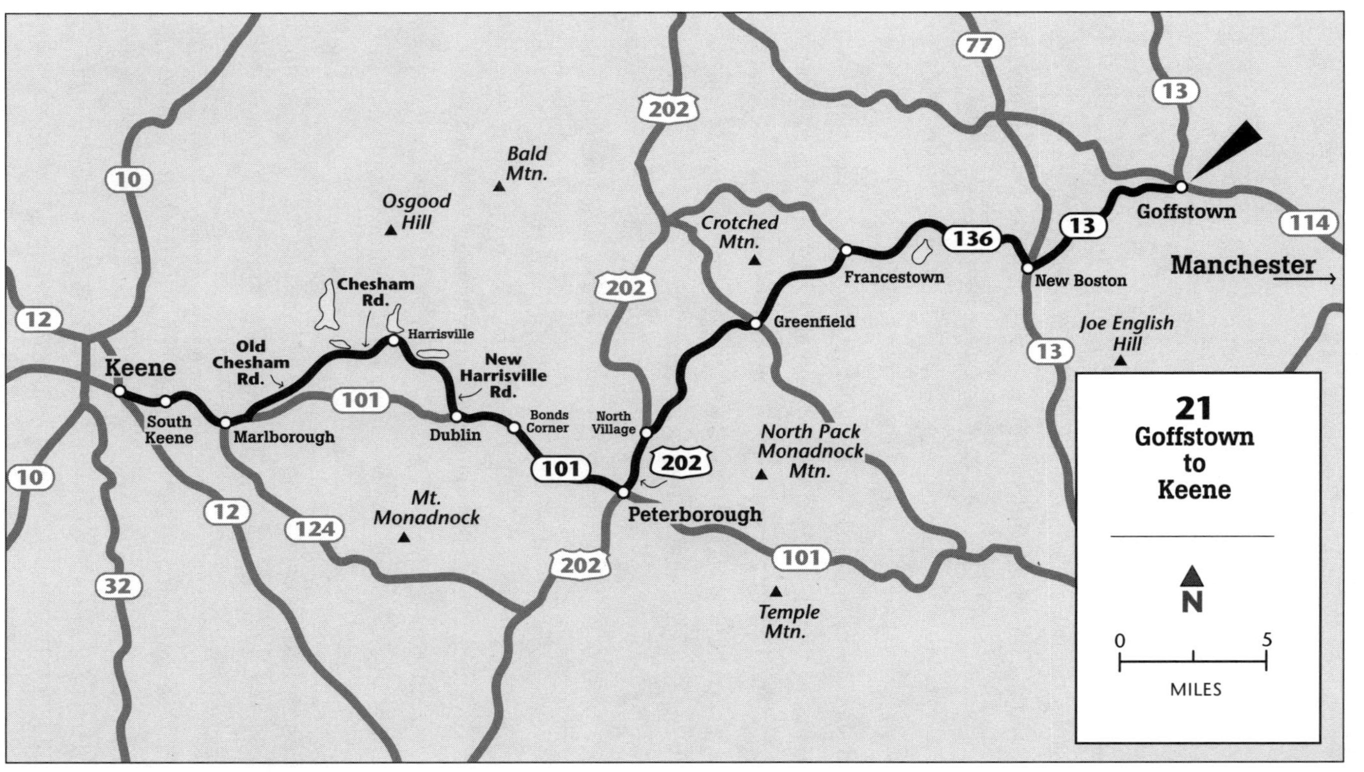
21
Goffstown
to
Keene
N
0
5
MILES
Goffstown
Manchester
New Boston
Joe English Hill
Francestown
Greenfield
Crotched Mtn.
North Pack Monadnock Mtn.
Temple Mtn.
North Village
Peterborough
Bonds Corner
Dublin
New Harrisville Rd.
Harrisville
Chesham Rd.
Old Chesham Rd.
Osgood Hill
Bald Mtn.
Mt. Monadnock
Marlborough
South Keene
Keene
13
114
77
136
202
101
124
12
10
32

south by McGregors Pond and following Meadow Brook, you pass the hill on your left just two miles south of and below the intersection. This rise is best examined from its south side, where it is faced with a striking precipice of bold rock. In the early 1700s, Joe English, grandson of the Agawam sachem Wasconnomet, was friendly with white settlers, amongst whom he was well known for his hunting and fighting prowess. Other Indians were resentful and suspected that Joe English was providing information about their movements and councils to the settlers. One night he was ambushed by his fellow tribesmen; he ran to the hill, ascending rapidly to escape death. Staying just far enough ahead of his murderous pursuers, he lured them over the mountain's summit, then he hid behind a boulder. The pursuers raced past English and plunged off the cliff, crashing to the rocks below.

After returning to the crossroads, you head west on NH 136 as it winds past hidden Haunted Lake to Francestown. The road quickly becomes rural and sparsely settled once out of the villages. Staying on NH 136 at the junction with NH 47, you drop farther westward to Greenfield on a winding course, crossing Rand Brook as you come into town. Crossing NH 31 in Greenfield at seventeen and a half miles from Goffstown, you turn more southwest in rural hill country with views southwest toward Grand Monadnock and northwest toward Skatutakee Mountain, in Hancock. North Pack Monadnock, Pack Monadnock, and Temple Mountain are visible to the southeast.

These lands are still dotted with small hill farms, some modernized, some abandoned. In these rural households, New Hampshire country life endured. Before the modern age, living in such places led to domestic scenes that were less than tranquil. A story is told of

The mill pond at hidden Harrisville

the mulish Hillsborough County farmer who took a fancy pitcher to get some cider out of the cellar barrel. Going downstairs to fetch the cider, he fell and tumbled down the steps in a rattling heap, shouting with pain. His wife, ever concerned with her possessions and not much with him, hollered, "Did you break that lovely pitcher?" To which he replied, furious at her unconcern for his battered state, "No, but I will, dammit!" and promptly smashed the pitcher against the chimney.

As you drift southwest, the road is hilly and winding, and there is little traffic. With the river still with you, join US 202 in North Village shortly, go left at the foot of a hill, and enter Peterborough. This pretty village provides a number of interesting diversions, for which you may wish to break your journey. The town is the site of the Monadnock Music Festival in July and August. (See Route

#16, page 123, for additional commentary on Peterborough.) The main streets of town are across the bridge and to the right as you approach the town center. Leave Peterborough from the south side of town by *going right* and *west* on NH 101. Drive through Bonds Corner by Mud Pond and shortly enter Dublin.

Up the hill in Dublin and thirty-four miles from Goffstown, *turn right* by the home of *Yankee Magazine* and climb the New Harrisville Road toward tiny Harrisville. After passing Skatutakee Lake, you arrive in this attractive former mill village, where the old buildings have been converted to modern usage. This is the home of Harrisville Designs, manufacturerer of fine wool yarns, and a mecca for weavers and knitters. After miles of forest travel, the sight of a complete red brick village, a remnant of another time, seems first to astonish. Harrisville is one of those increasingly rare places where handsome industrial architecture has been preserved in a creative and appealing way. Walk around here to enjoy interesting scenes over the millpond and the persistence of old, weathered brick found in building after building.

From Harrisville, follow winding, hilly Chesham and Old Chesham Roads southwest past Chesham Pond toward nearby Marlborough. The narrow way twists south of Kidder and Horse Hills. A side road will take you right and north to the Apple Hill Center for Chamber Music in Nelson. (Ask for directions locally.) After passing through Marlborough village, proceed right and west on NH 101 to South Keene and Keene. The journey ends once you reach NH 12 and 12A (Main Street). Turn right and ascend Main Street to a good selection of restaurants and stores.

22

Route:

Mount Sunapee–Newport Loop

Highway:

Routes 11, 103B, 103, local roads, Routes 31, 11

Distance:

50 miles (one way)

The quiet lake country of the Granite State's west-central region has long been a favorite destination of travelers not enamored of the honky-tonk precincts of Hampton Beach. Summer or winter, you can enjoy this beautiful, rolling countryside, dotted with hill farms, lakes, ponds, and low mountains. Two fine state parks are located here, too, and the water views are plentiful. Cozy inns await winter travelers, as does skiing on beautiful Mount Sunapee.

Begin at I-89, Exit 12, east of Georges Mills, an old crossroads settlement at the north end of Sunapee Lake. From I-89, go west and south through Georges Mills on NH 11 (Lake Avenue) by Otter Pond and Sunapee Lake's Herrick Cove, passing Mica Mine and Trow Hills. NH 11 drifts south around Brown and Garnett Hills and passes Dewey Beach, on the left. Enter Sunapee village and go left (east) on Central or Main Streets, covering the short distance to Sunapee Harbor. This busy harbor provides dockage and boat-launching facilities plus seasonal restaurants and accommodations.

Go back to NH 11 and *turn left*, then *bear left again* and *south* on NH 103B by the town hall. Continue uphill southward by Burkehaven Hill and Fishers Bay. Mountain ski trails are visible ahead on the high horizon. This road shortly brings you to a junction with NH 103, opposite lovely Mount Sunapee State Park. The 2,700-foot mountain is a major ski area in winter and offers rides on the ski lift in summer. Ask locally about hiking opportunities, too.

The landing at Sunapee Harbor

Go left and *east* on NH 103 here, and continue along the southern reaches of Sunapee Lake to the town of Newbury, where there is a small public beach. Proceeding on 103, you soon pass attractive Lake Todd on the left, then enter Bradford. Watch for a junction here with NH 114 (Center Road, becoming Sunset Hill Road), where you *bear right* and cross the West Branch of the Warner River on the covered Bement Bridge, about twelve miles south of Sunapee Harbor.

After going through the bridge, you will climb Center Road along Hoyt Brook to Bradford Center, then encounter some winding backcountry roads that will require all your attention and navigational skills. Here's what to do: At Bradford Center, on Center Road, you will come to a crossing with a small wooden signpost. *Go right* here

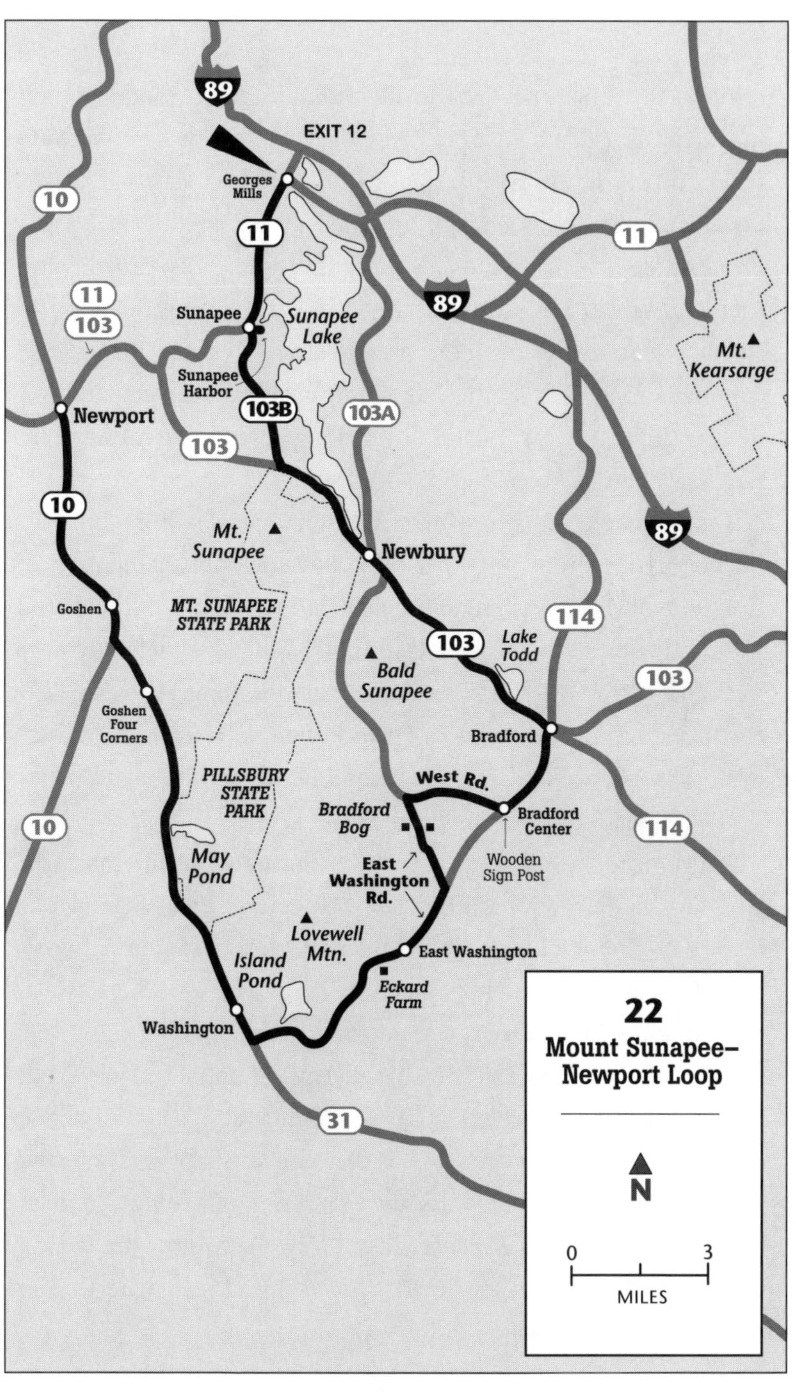

89
EXIT 12
Georges Mills
10
11
11
103
Sunapee
Sunapee Lake
Sunapee Harbor
103B
103A
11
89
Mt. Kearsarge
Newport
103
10
Mt. Sunapee
Newbury
89
Goshen
MT. SUNAPEE STATE PARK
114
103
Lake Todd
Bald Sunapee
103
Goshen Four Corners
Bradford
PILLSBURY STATE PARK
West Rd.
Bradford Bog
Bradford Center
114
10
May Pond
East Washington Rd.
Wooden Sign Post
Lovewell Mtn.
East Washington
Island Pond
Eckard Farm
Washington
31
22
Mount Sunapee–Newport Loop
N
0
3
MILES

on West Road. Stay on West Road, with occasional good views off to the northeast in high wooded country. Watch for East Washington Road on your left shortly, and *turn left* here. East Washington Road dips south through a series of lowlands, all part of the extensive Bradford Bog, which roams for miles in this area. The road climbs again, and there are occasional views of surrounding hills to the l eft. One sees few houses here, and an atmosphere of unspoiled countryside prevails on this alternately paved and gravel-surfaced road. Watch your turns carefully, making sure to always stay on East Washington Road.

A little more than twenty miles from Sunapee Harbor, you cross the county line from Merrimack to Sullivan County in dense woods. Continue on East Washington Road as it meanders southwest and west and comes to a crossroads in East Washington, where you *go right* and *west* at the site of a tumbledown building. As the road travels through the rocky fields of Eckard Farm, *keep left* and, farther *west*, pass Island Pond and Freezeland Pond, then come to a junction with NH 31 in Washington.

You *go right* and *northwest* on NH 31 through Washington, with its attractive Congregational Church, Washington Center School, and town hall. The road runs up Codman Hill and comes to Pillsbury State Park at Bean Mountain and May Pond. Campsites are available at the park, which borders a scenic pond. This inviting run through isolated hill country carries you farther north on NH 31 between Kennedy Hill and Bryant and Goves Mountains.

Here and there, this area reveals the remnants of old farms now going back to woods. This has always been tough country in which to put down roots. The tilled fields of New Hampshire are made of mean, rocky stuff, and for decades it was notoriously hard to gain

The Congregational Church, Washington Center School and Town Hall, Washington

a living from them. Once, it is said, a visiting preacher stopped here to watch a farmer successfully harvesting his rocky five acres. The clergyman remarked to the farmer: "You and God have certainly done a fine bit of work here." To which the farmer responded, "Wal, I dunno. You shoulda seen the place when just God was workin' it."

Proceed north now through Goshen Four Corners. These precincts sport signs that warn of moose crossings—not surprising when you observe the boggy ponds and streams that lie along the road. Drive cautiously. You join NH 10 in Goshen and follow this road up the map into the village of Newport, which nestles in a bend of the Sugar River.

You may end your journey here, or, if you wish, you can return to Sunapee Lake by traveling east from Newport on NH 11 and 103 through Guild and Wendell, where you *keep left* and east on NH 11 to return to Sunapee village, completing the loop.

Acknowledgments

An Author's Favorites

When you travel a lot, however beautiful the surroundings, the thought of a welcoming place to rest your head come nightfall assumes great importance. A fine breakfast can set up the day. A superb dinner may cap a wonderful odyssey over country roads. While traveling the several thousand miles requisite to completing this book, I had the good fortune to lodge with many friends who saw to my comfort and made sure that at the end of the day I could leave the road behind and often sit by a warm fire. I'd like to register my enthusiasm for their help and hospitality.

First, thanks to Lilly Myette, of the New Hampshire Department of Travel and Tourism, for efficient and helpful assistance on many occasions.

In far northern New Hampshire, my days in the Connecticut Lakes region were a treat at Betty Falton's **The Glen**, on First Connecticut Lake. A fine old sporting lodge with marvelous views across the big waters to the mountains of Maine, The Glen offered comfortable, rustic accommodations and excellent meals that left me reluctant to move on. That I could use my trout rod right at the lodge's front door didn't hurt, either. Absolute quiet, except for the occasional chatter of a loon, made sleep come early. Betty is a marvelous host of the old school variety and left me feeling pampered. Ask Betty about the winter they had 320 inches of snow here. Lakeside accommodations in the grand, old north country manner, that's The Glen. [The Glen, US 3, Pittsburg, New Hampshire. Tel. (603) 538-6500 or (800) 445-GLEN.]

In the western White Mountains, Mike and Pat McGuinn have brought **The Beal House Inn** back to life on Littleton's West Main Street. Two pleasant sitting rooms full of collected objects, part antique, part whimsy, offer a hideout until dinner arrives in the pleasant tavern dining room. Pat does the cooking with flair, and Mike makes sure that guests are thoroughly comfortable. Seven inviting guest rooms capture the flavor of this old place as it once was, but with present-day comforts. In winter, you can cut your own Christmas tree in the nearby hills, then enjoy dinner and an evening before the fireplace, with large doses of contentment. An excellent base for exploring the western White Mountains and upper Connecticut River region. [The Beal House Inn, West Main Street,

Beal House Inn, Littleton

The Shaker Inn at the Great Stone Dwelling

Littleton, New Hampshire. Tel. (603) 444-2661, Fax (603) 444-6224, or www.bealhouseinn.com.]

If you're traveling in the White Mountains with a family, the convenience and amenities of a large, well-run hostelry may suit you. Just west of the Shelburne Birches, the Labnon family's **Town and Country Motor Inn** in Shelburne, at the head of the eastern slopes of the White Mountains, offers all the services and convenience of a fully equipped motor hotel. The Town and Country's own dining room, lounge, pool, and golf course are convenient, and the facility is close to shops and stores in nearby downtown Gorham. [The Town and Country Motor Inn, US 2, Shelburne, New Hampshire. Tel. (603) 466-3315.]

In the Hanover-Lebanon area, travelers will enjoy, as do I, the unique environment of the inn at the Shaker Village on Mascoma Lake in Enfield. Operated by Historic Inns of New England, **The Shaker Inn at the Great Stone Dwelling** of the Lower Shaker

Village, on NH 4A, offers twenty-four comfortable period rooms in the largest "dwelling house" created by the Shaker sect in America. Furnished in the Shaker style, the lovely, austere accommodations reflect the simplicity of the Shaker movement. A comfortable dining room and tavern dispense good food and drink. The adjacent Shaker Museum interestingly captures the history of those who made this their "chosen vale" in 1793. Two shops carry Shaker products and books on Shaker history, and Shaker-style reproduction furniture is made next door by local craftsmen. A varied and extensive program of events, special weekends, and workshops augments the "things to do" list for those who stay at The Shaker Inn. A 2,500-acre nature preserve embraces the inn's hill country across the road, with guided hikes and cross-country skiing from the inn door. The last Shakers left this site in 1923, but the inn and museum keep the quality and art of the Shaker tradition alive and well. [The Shaker Inn at the Great Stone Dwelling, 447 Route 4A, Enfield, New Hampshire 03748. Tel. (603) 632-7810 or (888) 707-4257 or email info@theshakerinn.com.]

The Inn at Valley Farms

In southwestern New Hampshire, you'll find **The Inn at Valley Farms,** in Walpole, to be a welcoming place, with hosts Jacqui and Dane Badders. This fine old farm settlement, complete with red silos, was built in 1774. The double-chimney old inn offers attractively decorated rooms and superb breakfasts in a comfortable dining room. A solarium, cozy library, gardens, and nature trails provide relaxed diversion. Some of the produce is raised on the farm, and you're likely to find homemade maple syrup on your breakfast table. Jacqui, herself a craftswoman with local roots, will point you toward area galleries, exhibitions, craft shows, and historical attractions. Both downhill and cross-country skiing are close by in New Hampshire, and in Vermont, too.

Two cottages on the inn grounds may be rented and are sometimes the site of workshops or crafts demonstrations. A wonderful antidote to travel congestion and baleful, homogenized accommodations, The Inn at Valley Farms reflects great care in its restoration and makes a blissfully quiet haven from which to explore all of Cheshire County. Ask Jacqui to tell you the story of Madame Cheri. [The Inn at Valley Farms, RR 1, Box 280, Wentworth Road, Walpole, New Hampshire 03608. Tel. (603) 756-2855, e-mail www.innatvalleyfarms.com.]

Appendix A

State Parks and Campgrounds

The state of New Hampshire, besides being home to the vast White Mountain National Forest, has sixty-nine state parks and state forests. These range from small rest and picnic sites in scenic woodlands to beautiful campgrounds beside lakes and streams, to unusual perches such as Tip Top House on Mount Washington's summit. Seventeen of the state parks offer excellent camping facilities, and a number of these campgrounds are on or close to routes described in this book.

Parks with camping include:

Bear Brook State Park, off Route 28, Allenstown. (603) 485-9869

Cannon Mountain RV Park, Route 18, Franconia. (603) 823-8800

Coleman State Park, Little Diamond Pond Road, Stewartstown. (603) 538-6965

Deer Mountain Campground, Route 3, Pittsburg. (603) 538-6965

Dry River Campground, Route 302, Harts Location. (603) 374-2272

Ellacoya RV Campground, Route 11, Gilford. (603) 293-7821

Greenfield State Park, Route 136, Greenfield. (603) 547-3497

Hampton Beach RV Campground, Route 1A, Hampton. (603) 926-8990

Lafayette Campground, I-93 and Route 3, Franconia. (603) 823-9513

Lake Francis State Park, River Road off Route 3, Pittsburg. (603) 538-6965

Mollidgewock State Park, Route 16, Errol. (603) 482-3373

Monadnock State Park, Route 124, Jaffrey. (603) 532-8862

Moose Brook State Park, Jimtown Road off Route 2 West, Gorham. (603) 466-3860

Pawtuckaway State Park, Route 156, Nottingham. (603) 895-3031

Pillsbury State Park, Route 31, Washington. (603) 863-2860

Umbagog Lake Campground, Route 26, Cambridge. (603) 482-7795

White Lake State Park, Route 16, Tamworth. (603) 323-7350

For additional information on all New Hampshire state parks and forests, see the descriptive brochure with map listing state parks and campgrounds that is available from:

The New Hampshire Division of Parks and Recreation
172 Pembroke Road, P.O. Box 1856
Concord, New Hampshire 03302-1856
e-mail: info@nhparks.state.nh.us

Reservations for stays at New Hampshire state campgrounds during the mid-May to mid-October season may be made by calling (603) 271-3628.

Appendix B

Traveler Information

Regional centers offering information or assistance to travelers are spread around the state. Some of the most important points of contact are listed below. Call ahead for information.

General Information

New Hampshire weekly events, (800) 258-3608
New Hampshire Office of Travel and Tourism, (603) 271-2665
New Hampshire Department of Fish and Game, (603) 271-3421
New Hampshire Department of Forests and Lands, (603) 271-2215
New Hampshire Lodging and Restaurant Association, (603) 228-9585
New Hampshire Division of Parks and Recreation, (603) 271-3556
New Hampshire travelers' weather, (603) 225-5191
New Hampshire fall foliage reports, (800) 258-3608
New Hampshire road conditions, (800) 918-9993
Ski New Hampshire, (800) 88-SKI-NH
New Hampshire cross-country ski conditions, (800) 262-6660
New Hampshire alpine ski conditions, (800) 258-3608

Northern New Hampshire

Connecticut Lakes Tourist Association, (603) 538-7405

Connecticut Lakes Region, (603) 538-7118

Dixville Notch Information Center, (603) 255-4255

Northern White Mountains, (603) 752-6060 or (800) 992-7480

Lakes Region

Lakes Region Association, (603) 774-8664 or (888) 925-2537

Merrimack Valley Region

Concord Area Chamber of Commerce, (603) 224-2508

Manchester Area Chamber of Commerce, (603) 666-6600

Monadnock Region

Monadnock Travel Council, (603) 355-8155 or (800) 432-7864

Lake Sunapee Business Association, (603) 763-2495 or (800) 258-3530

White Mountains Region

White Mountains attractions, (603) 745-8720 or (800) FIND MTNS

Franconia Chamber of Commerce, (603) 823-5661 or (800) 237-9007

Lincoln-Woodstock Chamber of Commerce, (603) 745-6621 or (800) 227-4191

Jackson Chamber of Commerce, (603) 383-9356 or (800) 866-3334

Seacoast Region

Portsmouth Chamber of Commerce, (603) 436-1118

Exeter Chamber of Commerce, (603) 772-2411

Western New Hampshire

Claremont Chamber of Commerce, (603) 543-1296

Hanover Chamber of Commerce, (603) 643-3115

Lebanon Chamber of Commerce, (603) 448-1203

New London Chamber of Commerce, (603) 526-6575

Appendix C

Fishing and Boating

The state of New Hampshire has designated a range of access points for fishing and boating. They are distributed about the state and provide access to both lake and river waters. Some sites are handicapped-accessible. A total of 209 access points have been officially designated, and they are listed in an official publication offered by the New Hampshire Department of Fish and Game. Information includes details such as location, waters accessed, acreage, parking availability, hours open, type of fishing, and dockage. A map is included showing all points of public water access in the state, many of which are on or close to routes described in this volume.

Request the *New Hampshire Boating and Fishing Public Access Map* from the New Hampshire Department of Fish and Game, Statewide Public Access Program, 2 Hazen Drive, Concord, New Hampshire 03301. Tel. (603) 271-2224 or www.wildlife.state.nh.us.

Appendix D

Outdoor Programs

For persons interested in enjoying planned outdoor programs while touring New Hampshire, the resources below are good starting points.

The *New Hampshire Audubon Society* sponsors and operates a number of seasonal programs suitable for outdoor enthusiasts. Contact the society's headquarters at 3 Silk Farm Road, Concord, New Hampshire 03301, Tel. (603) 224-9909, or on-line at www.nhaudubon.org. New Hampshire Audubon operates seasonal programs at:

The Amoskeag Fishways Learning Center, Manchester
Massabesic Audubon Center, Auburn
Newfound Audubon Centers, East Hebron
Prescott Farm Audubon Center, Laconia
Seacoast Science Center, Odiorne Point State Park, Rye
Silk Farm Audubon Center, Concord

The *Appalachian Mountain Club,* NH Route 16, Gorham, New Hampshire, hosts a year-round program of outdoor workshops, first-aid training, nature-study programs, and guided hikes. A publication listing all workshops is available from the AMC's Education Department. For information on guided walks at Pinkham Notch, call (603) 466-2721. For the full program catalog, call (617) 523-0636, ext. 356, or on-line contact ekrabin@amcinfo.org.

The New Hampshire chapter of the *Sierra Club* offers field hikes and other outdoor program events at various locations. For information, write the group at 3 Bicentennial Square, Concord, New Hampshire 03301, or call (603) 224-8222.